Money on Autopilot

Your Step-by-Step Guide to Earning Money While You Sleep

Aline Szpaller

2024

United States of America

Money on Autopilot

Your Step-by-Step Guide to Earning Money While You Sleep

by Aline Szpaller

Copyright © 2024 by Aline Szpaller

All rights reserved.

No part of this book may be reproduced, distributed, or transmitted in any form or by any means, including photocopying, recording, or other electronic or mechanical methods, without the prior written permission of the publisher, except in the case of brief quotations embodied in critical reviews and certain other non-commercial uses permitted by copyright law.

Printed in the United States of America

First Edition: November 2024

This book is intended to provide helpful and informative material on the subjects addressed. It is not a substitute for professional advice, whether medical, legal, financial, or otherwise. The author and publisher disclaim any liability for the decisions you make based on the information contained in this book. Please consult the appropriate professionals for advice on your specific situation.

Dedication

To everyone who dreams of financial freedom and living life on their own terms. This book is for you.

To those who dare to believe in a better financial future—may this guide inspire your journey.

Dedicated to the dreamers, doers, and risk-takers who strive for freedom beyond the 9-to-5.

To my family, whose unwavering support made this journey possible, and to my readers, who inspire me to share what I have learned.

For my loved ones, who taught me the value of persistence and patience. This book is a testament to that wisdom.

To my children—may you grow up knowing the power of financial independence and the importance of chasing your dreams.

To the person who feels stuck and needs a way out—this is your roadmap to freedom.

To everyone who has ever believed there is more to life than trading time for money—this book is for you.

For those who are ready to take control of their future and build the life they deserve."

To the readers who inspire me to write and share ideas—your belief in possibilities drives everything I do.

Aline Szpaller

Table of Contents

Preface 9
Introduction 11
1. What is Passive Income? 13
2 Why Passive Income Matters Now More Than Ever 18
3 Types of Passive In Streams 22
4 Assessing Your Starting Point 28
5 Creating Your Passive Income Plan 34
6 Diversifying Your Passive Income Portfolio 50
7 Overcoming Challenges and Pitfalls in Passive Income 63
8 Future-Proofing Your Passive Income Portfolio 74
9 Debunking Myths About Passive Income 89
10 Overcoming Challenges on Your Passive Income Journey 94
11 Passive Income and Financial Freedom 98
12 Creating Your Personalized Income Blueprint 109
13 Mastering Patience and Persistence 117
Final Thoughts: Embracing the Journey to Financial Freedom 122
Acknowledgments 126
Frequently Asked Questions (FAQ) 127
Glossary of Terms 134
Appendix: Resources for Further Learning 137
Bibliography and References 139

PREFACE

If you are holding this book, chances are you are looking for a way to take control of your financial future. I have been there—working long hours, wondering if there was more to life than trading my time for money. I used to think financial freedom was just a dream, something reserved for the lucky few. But then I discovered the power of passive income, and it changed my life.

I wrote this book because I know how overwhelming it can feel to start building something from scratch. There is so much information out there, and not all of it is helpful or easy to apply. My goal is to simplify the process and show you that passive income is not just possible—it is achievable for anyone willing to put in the work upfront.

This book is for beginners and dreamers, for the nine-to-fivers who crave freedom, and for those who want to secure their future without sacrificing their present. Inside, I will share practical strategies, real-life examples, and actionable steps to help you create income streams that work for you, even when you are not working.

Building passive income takes time, effort, and patience. But if you stay committed, the results can transform your life. This book is not about get-rich-quick schemes; it is about creating a sustainable, scalable approach to financial freedom.

Whether you are just starting out or looking to expand your current efforts, I hope this book serves as a valuable guide on your journey. Let us get started on building the life you have always dreamed of.

— *Aline Szpaller.*

INTRODUCTION

Imagine waking up in the morning and knowing that, while you were sleeping, your money was working for you. Bills are being paid, savings are growing, and you have the freedom to spend your time on what truly matters—whether that is traveling, spending time with loved ones, or pursuing your passions. This is the promise of passive income.

For years, the traditional approach to earning money has revolved around one concept: exchanging time for a paycheck. While this can provide stability, it often comes at a cost—stress, burnout, and little time left for the things that bring us joy. I believe there is a better way. Passive income does not just offer financial freedom; it provides the most valuable currency of all—time.

But let me be clear: passive income is not about "easy money" or magical shortcuts to wealth. It requires effort, planning, and a willingness to step outside your comfort zone. The good news is that once you have built a solid foundation, those income streams can grow and sustain themselves with minimal input.

In this book, I'll walk you through the concept of passive income and why it is a notable change. Whether you are just starting to explore this idea or are ready to act, this guide will provide you with the tools and strategies you need to succeed.

You will learn:

- **What passive income is** (and what it is not), so you can focus on methods that actually work.

- **Proven strategies** to create income streams that suit your skills and interests.

- **Common pitfalls** to avoid on your journey toward financial independence.

- **How to scale and diversify** your income over time for long-term stability.

This book is more than just a how-to guide; it is an invitation to rethink your relationship with money and work. Whether you are aiming for complete financial independence or just looking to supplement your current income, this journey starts with a single step: deciding that your future is worth investing in.

Are you ready to break free from the paycheck-to-paycheck cycle?

Let us dive into the world of passive income and take that first step toward a more secure and fulfilling financial future!

1 What is Passive Income?

Money is one of the most essential resources in life, yet so many of us are taught only one way to earn it: by working a job and exchanging hours for a paycheck. This is known as **active income**—you work, you get paid. If you do not work, the income stops. It is the system most people are familiar with, but it is also limiting.

Passive income offers an alternative. Instead of constantly trading your time for money, passive income allows you to build systems, assets, or investments that generate money with minimal ongoing effort. It is about shifting your mindset from "I need to work to make money" to "I can make money work for me."

What Passive Income Looks Like in Real Life

Let me share a story about Sarah. Sarah is a teacher who loves her job but was frustrated with her stagnant income. She wanted to save for a house, but her salary barely covered her expenses. That is when she decided to explore passive income.

Sarah started small. She loved teaching, so she created a simple online course about effective classroom management and published it on a learning platform. At first, it was a lot of work—recording videos, designing materials, and marketing the course. But within a few months, she started earning a steady stream of income from her course sales.

Now, Sarah earns an extra $1,000 a month without having to do anything except answer occasional questions from students. Her course has given her a sense of financial freedom and allowed her to focus more on her passion for teaching.

Sarah's story is just one example of how passive income can change lives. Whether it is through creating content, investing, or building systems, the opportunities are endless.

Defining Passive Income

Passive income is often described as "money you earn while you sleep." While this phrase captures the essence of passive income, it is not entirely right. Passive income does not mean "no work"—it means **front-loading the effort** to create a stream of income that requires little to no maintenance in the future.

Examples of passive income include:

- **Royalties from a book or music:** Write it once and earn from it indefinitely.

- **Rental income from properties:** Purchase or manage a property, then earn from tenants.

- **Dividends from stocks:** Invest wisely and receive regular payouts.

- **Affiliate marketing on a blog or YouTube channel:** Create content that earns commissions over time.

Passive income contrasts with active income in its scalability. While active income is limited by the number of hours in a day, passive income has the potential to grow without requiring more of your time.

The Benefits of Passive Income

Why should you aim to build passive income streams? Here are some key reasons:

1. **Financial Freedom**

Passive income can provide you with a safety net, freeing you from reliance on a single job or paycheck. For example, Mark, a graphic designer, created and sold design templates online. Over time, his templates became a reliable source of income, allowing him to cut back on client work and focus on projects he truly enjoyed.

2. **Time Flexibility**

By reducing your dependency on active income, you gain more time to spend on what truly matters—whether that's pursuing hobbies, spending time with loved ones, or simply enjoying life.

3. **Scalability**

Once a passive income stream is set up, it can grow without requiring more of your time or energy. For example, an author who publishes a book on Amazon can earn royalties for years with minimal updates.

4. **Diversification**

Passive income allows you to spread your financial risk. Instead of relying on one source of income, you can create multiple streams that protect you during economic downturns.

Common Myths About Passive Income

Before diving into the specifics of how to create passive income, it is important to address a few misconceptions:

1. **"Passive Income Means No Work"**

Truth: Passive income requires effort upfront. Think of it like planting a garden: you invest time and energy to prepare the soil, plant the seeds, and water them. But once the plants grow, they provide fruits or vegetables with minimal effort.

2. **"It's Only for the Wealthy"**

Truth: Anyone can start building passive income, regardless of financial background. For instance, John started a blog with no upfront investment other than his time. Within two years, he was earning enough from ad revenue and affiliate marketing to quit his job.

3. **"It's a Get-Rich-Quick Scheme"**

Truth: Passive income is a long-term strategy. While it can lead to significant earnings, it requires patience and consistency to see results.

Your Passive Income Journey Starts Here

Building passive income starts with three key principles:

1. **Use Your Strengths**

Think about what you are good at or passionate about. For example, if you are an artist, you could sell digital prints. If you are a writer, consider creating e-books. Start with what you know and enjoy.

2. **Embrace Automation**

The secret to passive income is automation. Whether it is setting up automated payments for rental properties or creating digital products that sell on their own, automation is what makes passive income sustainable.

3. **Think Long-Term**

Passive income is not about instant gratification. It is about creating something now that will pay off in the future. Imagine building a bridge: it takes time and effort, but once it is complete, you can cross it anytime.

Conclusion

Passive income is not just about money—it is about freedom. It is the freedom to spend your time how you choose, to reduce financial stress, and to pursue your dreams without worrying about a paycheck.

As you read the upcoming chapters, I encourage you to keep an open mind and think about how the strategies can fit into your life. Whether you are starting from nothing or looking to expand your current efforts, this journey is one that has the potential to transform your life.

Are you ready to take the first step toward financial freedom?

Let us dive in!

2 Why Passive Income Matters Now More Than Ever

The world is changing rapidly. Traditional ideas about work, savings, and retirement are being challenged by shifts in the economy, technology, and global events. The days of relying solely on a single paycheck or a stable corporate job are becoming a thing of the past. If you want financial security, adaptability, and freedom, building passive income streams is no longer a luxury—it is a necessity.

The Modern Financial Reality

Let us start with some hard truths:

- **Jobs Are not as Secure as They Used to Be.** Even once-stable industries are now prone to layoffs, outsourcing, and automation. For example, roles like cashiers, drivers, and even writers are being replaced by AI and technology.

- **The Rising Cost of Living.** Inflation, housing costs, and healthcare expenses are outpacing income growth in many parts of the world.

- **Traditional Retirement is Fading.** Pensions are disappearing, and many people find they have not saved enough for retirement. Passive income can act as a safety net when traditional retirement savings fall short.

Passive income offers a way to navigate these uncertainties. By creating multiple streams of income, you can protect ever yourself from financial instability and create a cushion for the future.

Why Now is the Best Time to Start

If you are wondering, "Why should I start building passive income now?" here is why:

1. **Technology Makes It Easier Than Ever.**

    • With platforms like Amazon, Etsy, and YouTube, anyone can create and sell products or content globally.

    • Automated tools like email marketing, payment systems, and social media make it easy to scale passive income streams with minimal ongoing effort.

2. **The Gig Economy is Growing.**

    • Side hustles and freelance work are becoming the norm. While these often start as active income, many can evolve into passive income sources.

    • For instance, freelance graphic designers can create and sell design templates online, earning while they sleep.

3. **Global Audiences are Accessible.**

    • Never before has it been so easy to reach people around the world. A single digital product can be sold to thousands of people across different countries.

4. **Compounding Opportunities.**

    • The earlier you start; the sooner you can take advantage of compounding. Whether it is reinvesting earnings from stock dividends or reinvesting profits from a rental property, compounding helps passive income grow exponentially over time.

How Passive Income Changed Lives

Example 1: Michelle, the Blogger

Michelle was a stay-at-home mom who started a blog to document her parenting journey. Over time, she built an audience and began earning through affiliate marketing and sponsored posts. Today, her blog generates $5,000 a month in passive income, allowing her to contribute to her family's finances without sacrificing time with her kids.

Example 2: Raj, the Real Estate Investor
Raj worked in IT and used his savings to purchase a duplex. He rented out one side while living in the other, earning enough rental income to cover his mortgage. Over a few years, he purchased additional properties, and now his rental income exceeds his living expenses.

The Psychological Benefits of Passive Income

Passive income is not just about money—it is also about peace of mind. Imagine waking up and knowing your bills are covered, even if you decide to take a break or pursue something new. This kind of financial security reduces stress, increases confidence, and gives you the freedom to focus on what truly matters.

Many people describe the shift to passive income as life-changing. They no longer feel chained to a paycheck or afraid of financial setbacks. Instead, they feel empowered, knowing they have multiple safety nets in place.

Why You Should not Wait

It is tempting to think, "I'll start building passive income when I have more time or money." But the truth is, there is never a "perfect" time to start. The earlier you begin, the more time you must experiment, learn, and grow your income streams.

Remember, building passive income is a long-term investment. The time and effort you put in now can pay off for years—or even decades—to come.

What's Ahead

In the next chapter, we will dive into specific types of passive income streams. Whether you are a creative looking to monetize your skills, a professional seeking investment opportunity, or someone just starting out, there is a method that fits your goals and resources.

The journey may feel daunting at first, but it is one of the most rewarding investments you can make in yourself and your future. Let us explore the options and find the path that is right for you.

3 TYPES OF PASSIVE IN STREAMS

Not all passive income is created equal. What works for one person may not work for another, depending on your skills, resources, and goals. The good news is there are plenty of options to choose from, and you do not have to rely on just one. In fact, the most successful people in the passive income world diversify their income streams to reduce risk and maximize returns.

This chapter will introduce you to some of the most popular types of passive income, explain how they work, and help you identify which might be the best fit for you.

1. Investment-Based Passive Income

Investment-based passive income involves putting your money to work for you. This type of income typically requires upfront capital but can offer consistent, long-term returns.

Examples:

- Dividends from Stocks

By investing in dividend-paying stocks, you can earn regular payouts from companies. For example, if you own shares of a company like Coca-Cola, you will receive a dividend for each share you own.

- Real Estate Investments

Owning rental properties is one of the most common ways to generate passive income. By renting out residential or commercial spaces, you can earn monthly rental income while your property appreciates in value over time.

- Peer-to-Peer Lending

Platforms like LendingClub and Prosper allow you to lend money to individuals or small businesses in exchange for interest payments.

2. Digital Products

Creating digital products is a fantastic way to leverage your skills or knowledge. Once created, these products can be sold repeatedly without additional effort.

Examples:

- E-Books

Writing an e-book on a topic you are passionate about or knowledgeable in can generate long-term income through platforms like Amazon Kindle Direct Publishing (KDP).

- Online Courses

Platforms like Udemy or Teachable allow you to create and sell courses on virtually any topic, from cooking to coding.

- Stock Photos or Videos

If you're a photographer or videographer, you can sell your work on platforms like Shutterstock or Adobe Stock.

3. Content-Based Passive Income

Content-based passive income focuses on creating value through blogs, YouTube channels, or podcasts. These require consistent effort upfront to build an audience but can generate income over time.

Examples:

- Blogging

By writing articles and monetizing your blog through ads, affiliate links, or sponsored posts, you can create a steady income stream.

- YouTube Channels

YouTube offers revenue through ad placements, memberships, and sponsorships. The more views and subscribers you gain, the more passive income you can earn.

- Affiliate Marketing

Promoting products or services and earning a commission for each sale is a generic form of content-based passive income. For instance, if you write a blog post reviewing a product and include an affiliate link, you will earn money whenever someone makes a purchase through that link.

4. Licensing and Royalties

If you are a creator or innovator, licensing and royalties can be a powerful way to generate income from your intellectual property.

Examples:

- Music and Art Royalties

Musicians and artists can earn royalties every time their work is used in media, sold, or streamed.

- Patents

Inventors can license their patents to companies in exchange for royalties.

- Software or Apps

Developers who create apps or software can earn ongoing income from downloads, subscriptions, or licensing deals.

5. Physical Products and Automation

While many passive income strategies focus on digital products, selling physical products can also become passive with the right systems in place.

Examples:

- **Amazon FBA (Fulfillment by Amazon)**

With Amazon FBA, you handle the product sourcing while Amazon takes care of storage, shipping, and customer service.

- **Print-on-Demand**

Platforms like Printful or Redbubble allow you to sell custom-designed products like t-shirts, mugs, and posters without worrying about inventory or shipping.

Choosing the Right Passive Income Stream

When deciding which passive income stream to pursue, consider the following:

- **Your Skills and Interests**

What are you good at, or what do you enjoy? For example, if you are a talented writer, creating an e-book or blog might be a natural fit. If you are more visually inclined, you might prefer creating a YouTube channel or selling stock photos.

- **Your Available Resources**

Do you have upfront capital to invest, or are you starting with minimal funds? Investment-based passive income streams like real estate or stocks may require more money upfront, whereas digital products or content creation often require only your time and creativity.

- **Your Time Commitment**

Some passive income streams, like creating online courses or blogs, require significant effort upfront. Others, like dividend investing or peer-to-peer lending, involve less work initially but may take time to grow.

- **Your Long-Term Goals**

Are you looking for steady income to supplement your current job, or do you want to build something that could eventually replace your full-time income? Your goals will influence the types of streams you choose to pursue.

The Power of Combining Multiple Streams

While starting with one passive income stream is ideal, combining multiple streams can create a more robust and diversified financial future. For example:

- A blogger could combine ad revenue with affiliate marketing.

- A real estate investor might also invest in dividend stocks to balance their portfolio.

- A course creator could cross-sell e-books or premium coaching services.

Each income stream you add strengthens your financial foundation and reduces your reliance on any single source of income.

Overcoming Analysis Paralysis

It is easy to feel overwhelmed by the number of options available. You might wonder, "What if I pick the wrong one?" The truth is, there is no perfect starting point, and you can always pivot later.

Here is an effortless process to get started:

1. Pick One Stream. Start with what feels most achievable or exciting to you.

2. Learn and Experiment. Study successful examples, and take small steps to build your stream.

3. Adjust as You Go. If one method does not work, adapt or try something new. The key is to keep moving forward.

What's Next

Now that you understand the various types of passive income streams, it is time to roll up your sleeves and take action. In the next chapter, we will explore how to evaluate your current financial situation, identify opportunities, and set realistic goals for your passive income journey.

Remember, passive income is not about achieving perfection—it is about progress. Start small, stay consistent, and watch your efforts grow over time.

4 ASSESSING YOUR STARTING POINT

Before diving into creating passive income streams, it is important to take a step back and evaluate your current situation. Understanding where you stand financially, what skills you have, and what resources you can allocate will help you craft a realistic and achievable plan.

In this chapter, we will focus on assessing three key areas: your financial foundation, your personal skills and interests, and the time and effort you can commit to building passive income.

1. Understanding Your Financial Foundation

Your financial foundation is the starting point for any passive income journey. Knowing where you stand will guide the types of income streams that are possible for you.

Questions to Ask Yourself:

- **What is my current income and expense situation?**

Create a budget that outlines your monthly income, fixed expenses (like rent and utilities), and variable expenses (like dining out or entertainment).

- **Do I have savings to invest?**

Some passive income streams, like real estate or dividend stocks, require upfront capital. Knowing how much you can comfortably invest will help narrow down your options.

- **Am I carrying any high-interest debt?**

If you have high-interest debt, like credit card balances, consider focusing on paying it off first. The interest you are paying might outweigh any potential gains from passive income in the short term.

- **Do I have an emergency fund?**

A good rule of thumb is to have 3–6 months' worth of expenses saved before starting any risky ventures. This will give you peace of mind as you experiment with new income streams.

2. Identifying Your Skills and Interests

Passive income is often most successful when it aligns with your strengths and passions. This ensures that the initial effort feels rewarding rather than burdensome.

Steps to Identify Your Strengths:

1. **List Your Skills:** Think about what you are good at—writing, designing, teaching, analyzing data, or even creating crafts.

2. **List Your Hobbies and Interests:** What activities make you lose track of time? Consider hobbies like photography, baking, or fitness that could be monetized.

3. **Ask for Feedback:** Sometimes, friends and family can identify strengths you may overlook.

Examples of Aligning Skills with Passive Income:

- A graphic designer could create and sell templates on platforms like Canva.

- A fitness enthusiast might write an e-book about home workout plans.

- A data analyst could create and sell Excel templates or courses.

3. Assessing Your Time and Energy

Passive income requires effort upfront, so understanding how much time you can realistically dedicate is crucial.

Questions to Ask Yourself:

- **How many hours a week can I commit?**
Even 2–3 hours a week can make a difference if used consistently.

- **Am I willing to sacrifice leisure time temporarily?**
Building passive income may mean prioritizing long-term goals over short-term entertainment.

- **What motivates me to keep going?**
Having a clear "why"—whether it is financial freedom, more family time, or early retirement—can keep you motivated through challenges.

4. Setting Clear Goals

Once you have assessed your finances, skills, and time, it is time to set realistic goals. Start small and build momentum as you learn and grow.

Short-Term Goals:

- Choose one passive income stream to start with.

- Dedicate a specific number of hours each week to building your stream.

- Aim for a small initial target, like earning $100 in your first month.

Long-Term Goals:

- Diversify your income streams.

- Increase your monthly passive income to a specific amount (e.g., $1,000/month).
- Replace a portion—or all—of your active income.

5. Overcoming Common Challenges

Starting can be intimidating, especially if you are unfamiliar with the process. Here are a few common challenges and how to address them:

- **Fear of Failure:**

Remember, failure is part of the process. Each setback teaches you something valuable for future success.

- **Lack of Knowledge:**

Use free or low-cost resources like YouTube, blogs, or courses to build your understanding.

- **Impatience:**

Passive income takes time to grow. Focus on consistent effort rather than instant results.

Advanced Passive Income Strategies

Once you have built a few basic streams of passive income, it is time to consider expanding into more advanced strategies.

Real Estate Syndications

Real estate syndications allow investors to pool resources and invest in larger, more lucrative real estate projects. You contribute a smaller amount of capital and, in return, you get a share of the profits. This is an excellent way to gain exposure to larger properties without the upfront capital required for direct ownership.

Building and Selling Digital Assets

If you have built an online business or developed a popular blog, you can sell that asset once it becomes profitable. Websites, e-commerce stores, and even entire social media accounts can be sold for a significant profit.

Leveraging Technology for Automation

Technology is your best friend when it comes to automating tasks and freeing up time. Here are some tools to consider:

Automated Marketing

Email marketing platforms like **Mailchimp** and **ConvertKit** can automate your email campaigns, drip sequences, and follow-ups. Similarly, social media scheduling tools like **Buffer** and **Hootsuite** let you automate posts, saving you time and ensuring consistent engagement.

Real Estate Management Software

If you are managing rental properties, tools like **Cozy** or **TenantCloud** allow you to automate rent collection, maintenance requests, and tenant communications.

Pros and Cons of Passive Income Strategies

To help you better understand the advantages and potential drawbacks of each passive income strategy, here is a quick comparison chart:

Strategy	Pros	Cons
Rental Properties	Steady income, property appreciation	High upfront costs, maintenance required
Dividend Investing	Reliable income, low effort	Market volatility, requires capital

32

Blogging	Creative freedom, high earning potential	Slow to generate income, high upfront effort
Print-on-Demand	Low risk, scalable	Competitive market, relies on design skills
Online Courses	Recurring income, easy to scale	Time-intensive to create content
Digital Products	Passive once created, low overhead	Requires marketing, niche expertise

What's Next

Now that you have assessed your starting point, you are ready to take action. In the next chapter, we will guide you through creating a personalized plan to launch your first passive income stream. You will learn how to set up your stream, avoid common pitfalls, and start building momentum toward financial independence.

Remember, the journey to passive income is just that—a journey. It starts with understanding where you are today and taking the first step toward where you want to be tomorrow.

5 CREATING YOUR PASSIVE INCOME PLAN

Now that you have assessed your financial foundation, skills, time, and goals, it is time to take the next step: creating a detailed plan. A strong plan will guide you as you launch your first passive income stream and help you stay focused as you grow your earnings over time.

In this chapter, we will walk through how to create a clear, actionable plan that aligns with your resources, skills, and goals, with a strong emphasis on automation and scaling.

1. Choosing Your First Passive Income Stream

With so many options available, selecting the right passive income stream is crucial. As we discussed in Chapter 3, you should choose something that matches your current skills, interests, and available resources. But how do you actually narrow it down?

Steps to Choose the Best Stream for You:

1. **Review Your Financial Assessment**

Consider the amount of upfront capital you have. If you have savings to invest, stocks or real estate might be a good fit. If you are working with little or no savings, digital products, content creation, or affiliate marketing may be a more accessible start.

Example:
Suppose you have $10,000 to invest. You could use this for a down payment on a rental property, purchase dividend-paying stocks, or buy equipment to start a blog or YouTube channel. If you do not have savings, consider creating an

34

eBook or an online course. These options typically require little to no upfront cost.

2. Factor in Your Time Commitment

If you are only able to dedicate a few hours a week, focus on passive income streams that require less ongoing effort once they are set up. For example, writing an eBook or creating an online course may require significant time at first but can be mostly hands-off once they're created.

Example:
If you are working full-time and have a family, you may not have the time to manage a real estate portfolio or maintain an eCommerce store. However, you could spend a few hours a week researching topics for an eBook, writing it, and then uploading it to Amazon KDP, where it can generate income without much ongoing work.

3. Match to Your Interests and Skills

If you love teaching, creating an online course could be a great option. If you enjoy photography, selling stock photos may be a good fit. Choose something that excites you, as this will help you stay motivated when the going gets tough.

Example:
If you are an experienced marketer, you might consider creating an online marketing course. If you are a hobbyist photographer, you could sell stock photos on websites like Shutterstock or Adobe Stock. Aligning your skills with your income stream will make the process much more enjoyable and sustainable in the long run.

2. Setting Up Your Passive Income Stream

Once you have chosen your passive income stream, it's time to set it up. Here's how to approach it:

For Digital Products (eBooks, Courses, Printables, etc.):

1. Market Research:

Before creating anything, research your niche. Look at what's already available and identify gaps or areas where you can offer something unique. Read reviews, join online communities, and listen to what people are asking for.

Example:
Before writing an eBook about "Self-Improvement for Busy Professionals," you might research existing books on Amazon. Look for books that get good reviews but also find areas where they might be lacking, such as actionable tips, more specific examples, or a focus on people with limited time. Use this information to shape your own unique offering.

2. **Content Creation:**

Start creating your product. If you're writing an eBook, break it into chapters and outline your key points. For online courses, plan out the lessons and modules. If you're creating a printable or design, focus on high-quality and visually appealing content.

Example:
If you're creating an online course, break it into bite-sized lessons that are easy to consume. For instance, if your course is about personal finance, you could create modules on budgeting, saving, and investing, with accompanying worksheets and videos.

3. **Publishing/Platform Setup:**

Choose your platform for selling. Amazon Kindle Direct Publishing (KDP) is great for eBooks, while Teachable or Udemy are perfect for courses. If you're selling printables or designs, platforms like Etsy or Gumroad are great options.

Example:
If you've created a course on how to start a side hustle, you could use Teachable for course hosting. If you're selling eBooks, Amazon KDP is a great platform because it provides a vast audience. If you're selling a productivity planner, Etsy would be ideal due to its huge user base interested in creative and personal growth products.

4. **Marketing:**

Don't wait for your product to go live before you start building an audience. Leverage social media, blogging, and email marketing to generate interest. Create a website or landing page to collect email addresses, which can be used for future promotions.

Example:
Start a blog that provides tips on how to manage side hustles or achieve financial independence. Use this blog to promote your eBook or course. Collect emails from your readers so you can market directly to them. Promote your product on your social media channels to drive traffic to your blog or landing page.

3. Automating and Scaling Your Passive Income Stream

The beauty of passive income lies in automation. Once you've set up your stream, the next step is to automate as much of the process as possible. This reduces the amount of time you need to spend on the business, allowing it to grow passively.

Automation Tips:

1. **Use Marketing Automation Tools:**

Tools like **Mailchimp**, **ConvertKit**, and **ActiveCampaign** allow you to set up automated email sequences for nurturing leads and driving sales. Set up welcome emails for new subscribers, automatic sales follow-ups, and even email drip campaigns to promote new products or services. Once set up, these campaigns can run indefinitely, providing continuous engagement and conversions without further effort.

Example:
Suppose you're selling an eBook on personal finance. You could create an email sequence that starts with a welcome email, followed by a series of educational emails offering tips on budgeting and saving. At the end of the sequence, you can offer a discount on a more advanced course or another eBook you've created.

2. **Schedule Content:**
If you're running a blog or social media, batch-creating content and scheduling it in advance can save you a lot of time. **Buffer, Hootsuite**, and **Later** are excellent tools for scheduling posts on social media. Similarly, **WordPress** and **Medium** allow you to write and schedule blog posts. For YouTube, you can upload your videos in advance and schedule them for release, keeping your channel active even when you're not available to publish new content.

Example:
Let's say you run a blog about fitness and nutrition. Spend one weekend writing and scheduling a month's worth of blog posts and social media content. This way, even when you're busy with other things, your blog and social media will remain active, driving traffic and engagement without requiring daily work.

3. **Use E-Commerce Automation for Sales:**
If you're selling physical or digital products, consider using platforms that handle most of the sales process for you. **Etsy, Shopify, Gumroad**, and **Amazon** all manage the transaction, payment processing, and product delivery for you. This allows you to focus on creating more products while the platform takes care of the logistics.

Example:
If you're selling stock photography, sites like **Shutterstock** or **Adobe Stock** handle payment processing, licensing, and delivery. Once you upload your images, you don't have to do anything else—just collect royalties as people purchase your images.

4. **Outsource Tasks:**
As your passive income grows, consider outsourcing tasks that don't require your personal touch. Platforms like **Upwork, Fiverr**, or **Freelancer** allow you to hire virtual assistants, content writers, graphic designers, or even customer service agents. This allows you to focus on high-level strategies while the daily tasks are handled by experts.

Example:

You could hire a freelance writer to create blog posts or eBook content for you. Or, if you run a YouTube channel, hire a video editor to help with post-production. By outsourcing, you free up your time to focus on strategy and scaling.

5. **Create Recurring Revenue Streams:**

Some passive income streams can generate recurring revenue, meaning you'll earn money regularly without additional effort. Examples include:

- **Subscription Models** (e.g., Patreon or a membership site)

- **Affiliate Programs** that offer residual commissions (e.g., Amazon Associates, ClickBank)

- **Digital Subscription Boxes** (e.g., providing a monthly subscription of new digital tools, templates, or resources)

Example:
If you have an online course, you could offer a subscription service where members get access to exclusive content, monthly webinars, or Q&A sessions. Similarly, you could join affiliate programs related to your niche. For example, if you write about home improvement, you can join Amazon's affiliate program to earn commissions on products you recommend.

6. **Reinvest Earnings:**

To scale your passive income, reinvest a portion of the profits you generate. For example:

- Use profits from an eBook to create a series of related eBooks or a course on the same topic.

- Reinvest affiliate income into paid ads or influencer marketing to drive more traffic to your blog or website.

- Use earnings from a real estate investment to purchase additional properties or fund renovations that increase rental income potential.

Example:
Let's say your eBook on "Personal Finance for Millennials" is generating consistent income. Instead of just pocketing the money, reinvest it to create a companion online course on investing, or even launch a YouTube channel where you discuss finance-related topics. This reinvestment expands your brand, reaching a wider audience and generating more passive income.

7. **Test and Optimize Your Streams:**

As your passive income streams grow, it's important to test different strategies and optimize for better performance. Look at metrics like conversion rates, click-through rates, or engagement to determine which strategies work best. For instance, A/B testing your sales pages, email subject lines, or product offerings can help refine your approach.

Example:
If you are running an eCommerce store selling digital products, you might experiment with different pricing strategies or promotional offers. If your current eBook is priced at $14.99, you could test whether lowering the price to $9.99 or offering a bundle deal with other products increases sales. Keep track of the data, analyze the results, and continuously adjust your strategies.

4. Monitoring and Adjusting Your Passive Income Plan

Your passive income plan will require ongoing monitoring and adjustments. Even though the idea of passive income is that it's hands-off, you'll need to ensure your systems are running smoothly and that you're optimizing for growth. Here's how to stay on top of things:

1. **Track Your Metrics:**

Regularly check your sales, traffic, and engagement metrics. This will help you identify which streams are the most profitable and where to put your energy for maximum results.

Example:
If you're selling an online course, keep track of how many new students enroll each month, how much income you're generating, and your customer feedback. Similarly, if you're doing affiliate marketing, track the performance of each affiliate link and see which products are converting the best.

2. **Assess Long-Term Viability:**

Some passive income streams, like real estate or dividend stocks, may take longer to mature, but they can continue to provide income over a long period. Be sure to assess each stream's long-term potential and make adjustments as needed. For example, if a particular income stream is underperforming, it might be worth shifting resources to a more lucrative one.

Example:
You may find that your affiliate income from a particular program is decreasing. In this case, it might make sense to explore other affiliate programs with higher payouts or even start your own affiliate program to boost your income.

3. **Adapt to Market Changes:**

The digital landscape is constantly changing. Social media algorithms, advertising costs, and consumer behavior can all impact your passive income streams. Stay flexible and be ready to pivot. If one strategy isn't working, try another. Stay informed by following industry blogs, networking with others in your field, and continuing your education.

Example:
If you've been running Facebook ads to promote an eBook, but the cost per click has increased significantly, consider experimenting with other platforms like Google Ads or influencer marketing. Or if you're running a YouTube channel and the platform changes its algorithm, leading to decreased visibility, you might need to adjust your content strategy or even expand to new platforms like TikTok or podcasting.

4. **Scale When Ready:**
Once your passive income stream is generating a stable amount of income and you've optimized your process, it's time to scale. Scaling could mean increasing marketing efforts, expanding your product line, or investing in outsourcing to grow even more.

Example:
If you have a profitable eBook on "How to Invest in Real Estate with Little Money," you could scale by creating a series of eBooks on different real estate topics, such as "House Hacking for Beginners" or "Flipping Houses for Profit." Alternatively, you could offer a membership program that gives ongoing advice and resources for real estate investors.

Choosing the Right Passive Income Stream

Not all passive income opportunities suit everyone. Your goals, skills, lifestyle, and resources determine what works best for you. This chapter explores tailored passive income ideas for specific audiences, helping you find what aligns with your unique situation.

1. Passive Income for Students

Students often have limited time and capital but can leverage creativity and technology to build income streams.

Ideas for Students:

- **Create Digital Products:** Design study guides, flashcards, or course notes to sell on platforms like Gumroad or Etsy.

- **Start a YouTube Channel:** Share educational content, tutorials, or lifestyle vlogs and earn through ads and sponsorships.

- **Participate in Affiliate Marketing:** Promote products or services related to your niche (e.g., student tech or books) via blogs or social media.

Real-Life Example:
Sarah, a college sophomore, created a series of printable planners for students. Selling them on Etsy, she earned $500 monthly while balancing her studies.

2. Passive Income for Busy Professionals

Professionals often have higher incomes but limited time. Automation and investing are key strategies for this group.

Ideas for Professionals:

- **Invest in Dividend-Paying Stocks or ETFs:** Set up automated contributions to a diversified portfolio for consistent returns.

- **Create Online Courses:** Share your professional expertise through platforms like Udemy or Teachable.

- **Buy Rental Properties:** Use your income to acquire and manage real estate with the help of property management services.

Real-Life Example:
Mark, an accountant, created a course teaching small business owners about tax basics. His course generates over $1,000 monthly with minimal ongoing effort.

3. Passive Income for Stay-at-Home Parents

Stay-at-home parents often have flexible schedules but need income streams that can be managed from home.

Ideas for Stay-at-Home Parents:

- **Write Children's Books:** Self-publish on Amazon KDP and create stories inspired by your parenting experiences.

- **Sell Crafts or Printables:** Use platforms like Etsy to sell handmade items or digital downloads like chore charts and activity sheets.

- **Start a Blog or Podcast:** Focus on parenting tips, home organization, or meal planning and monetize through ads and affiliate marketing.

Real-Life Example:
Emily, a mother of two, designed chore trackers for kids. Selling them as printables on Etsy, she earns $600 monthly while managing her household.

4. Passive Income for Retirees

Retirees often have more time and financial resources to explore low-maintenance income streams.

Ideas for Retirees:

- **Invest in REITs (Real Estate Investment Trusts):** Earn regular dividends from real estate without the hassle of property management.

- **License Creative Work:** If you've written books, taken photos, or composed music, license your work to earn royalties.

- **Sell Expertise:** Offer consulting or coaching services and package them into e-books or courses.

Real-Life Example:
John, a retired teacher, wrote a series of e-books on effective teaching strategies. He now earns $800 monthly in passive income.

5. Passive Income for Hobbyists and Creatives

If you have a passion for art, music, writing, or any creative hobby, you can turn it into a source of income.

Ideas for Hobbyists:

- **Sell Photography or Art:** Use platforms like Shutterstock, Redbubble, or Etsy to sell digital downloads or prints.

- **Publish Fiction or Poetry:** Self-publish your stories or collections on Amazon KDP and earn royalties.

- **License Your Music:** Offer your compositions for use in commercials, films, or YouTube videos.

Real-Life Example:
Anna, a hobbyist photographer, uploaded her photos to stock photography sites. She now earns royalties every month without additional effort.

6. Passive Income for Tech-Savvy Individuals

If you are skilled in technology or coding, you can leverage those abilities for scalable passive income.

Ideas for Tech-Savvy Individuals:

- **Develop Mobile Apps:** Create utility apps or games and earn through ads or in-app purchases.

- **Build and Sell SaaS Products:** Create software-as-a-service platforms for recurring subscription income.

- **Design and Sell Website Themes or Plugins:** Offer solutions for WordPress or Shopify users.

Real-Life Example:

Jake, a programmer, created a budgeting app. With minimal maintenance, the app generates $2,000 monthly in passive income.

7. Passive Income for Adventure Seekers

For those who love to travel or seek unconventional lifestyles, passive income can support your adventures.

Ideas for Adventure Seekers:

- **Start a Travel Blog or Vlog:** Share your experiences and monetize through ads, sponsorships, and affiliate marketing.

- **Rent Out Your Home:** Use platforms like Airbnb to earn income while you're away.

- **Sell Travel Photography:** Capture and sell your photos to magazines, stock platforms, or tourism companies.

Real-Life Example:
Sam and Mia, travel enthusiasts, document their journeys on YouTube. Ad revenue and brand partnerships now fund their trips worldwide.

8. Passive Income for Aesthetic Lovers

If you have an eye for beauty and design, monetize your creative taste.

Ideas for Aesthetic Lovers:

- **Sell Print-on-Demand Products:** Create designs for clothing, home decor, or stationery.

- **Curate and Sell Digital Presets:** Offer Lightroom or video presets for photographers and content creators.

- **Create a Social Media Account:** Build a following on Instagram or Pinterest and monetize through collaborations or affiliate links.

Real-Life Example:
Lisa, an Instagram aesthetic curator, partnered with brands to feature their products, earning $1,500 monthly.

Key Takeaways

- Tailor your passive income strategy to your skills, lifestyle, and goals.

- Start small and scale as you gain experience and resources.

- Explore the opportunities that align with your passions and interests for greater fulfillment.

Comparing Popular Passive Income Streams

Passive Income Stream	Initial Investment	Time Commitment	Risk Level	Scalability
Rental Properties	High	Medium	Medium	High
Dividend Stocks	Medium to High	Low	Low	Medium
Print-on-Demand Business	Low to Medium	Low	Low	High
Blogging	Low	High (initially)	Low	High
Online Courses	Medium	Medium	Low	High
Digital Products (eBooks, PDFs)	Low	Low	Low	High

Interviews with Experts

I interviewed several successful entrepreneurs and passive income experts to share their best advice. Here is what they had to say:

Interview with John, Real Estate Investor

"Real estate is a powerful way to build wealth because it allows you to leverage debt to acquire properties that generate cash flow. The key is understanding your market and focusing on long-term appreciation, not short-term gains." – John, 45, a seasoned real estate investor with a portfolio of 20 properties.

Interview with Lisa, Affiliate Marketing Expert

"Affiliate marketing is a fantastic passive income model, but it takes time to build. Focus on creating content that adds value to your audience, and the sales will follow. Start small and scale as you learn." – Lisa, 32, a full-time affiliate marketer.

Conclusion of Chapter 5: Building Your Passive Income Empire

Creating a passive income stream is not something that happens overnight, but by following these steps and staying consistent, you can build a portfolio of income sources that grow with minimal active effort.

The key is to start small, automate as much as possible, and continuously scale and optimize your efforts. With persistence and the right mindset, you'll be on your way to achieving financial freedom through passive income.

In the next chapter, we will explore the concept of **"Diversifying Your Passive Income Portfolio"**, and how to reduce risk by creating multiple income streams.

6 Diversifying Your Passive Income Portfolio

Now that you have established a passive income stream or two, it's time to think about growing your financial portfolio and increasing your security by diversifying. Relying on one income source can be risky, and diversifying your passive income streams can help safeguard against sudden drops in earnings. Moreover, multiple income sources can work in harmony to amplify your profits.

In this chapter, we will explore how to diversify your passive income portfolio and offer more in-depth examples of the various options available. We will also go deeper into balancing high-risk and low-risk income streams, and how to monitor your portfolio's health for long-term success.

1. The Importance of Diversification

When it comes to passive income, diversification is not just about having multiple streams—it's about **mixing** streams with different levels of risk, returns, and time horizons to create a well-balanced portfolio.

Why Diversification is Essential:

- **Reduced Risk:** Just as with a stock portfolio, spreading your investments across various assets can lower your overall risk. In the world of passive income, relying on only one stream can expose you to significant losses if that stream fails or slows down.

- **Stable Cash Flow:** Different income streams have different patterns. For example, rental properties generate monthly income, while stocks might pay quarterly dividends. Having a mix of these can smooth out any gaps in cash flow.

- **Long-term Sustainability:** Some passive income streams, like eBooks or online courses, can lose steam over time, while others, like real estate or dividends, offer reliable income year after year. Diversifying ensures that you always have a reliable backup.

Example of Risk Reduction:
Imagine you have one property generating rental income. If a tenant moves out or there are unexpected repairs, that cash flow stops. But if you also have a blog that generates affiliate marketing income and a dividend stock portfolio, you'll still have income coming in while you handle the issues with the property. By diversifying, you ensure that a temporary setback in one area doesn't derail your financial progress.

2. Types of Passive Income Streams to Diversify With

Let's now take a deeper look at different categories of passive income streams that you can use to create a diversified portfolio.

A. Digital Products and Content

1. **Online Courses and Webinars**

The rise of e-learning has made online courses one of the most popular ways to generate passive income. Once the course is created, it can be sold repeatedly without much additional effort.

Further Example:
Imagine you're an expert in **social media marketing**. You can create a course teaching others how to run effective

Facebook ads or how to grow an Instagram following. You can host your course on platforms like **Udemy**, **Teachable**, or even your own website. Once set up, the course can sell to new customers every day without you having to create new content.

2. Ebooks and Digital Guides

Ebooks are one of the easiest and most straightforward ways to enter the world of passive income. Writing a book on a subject you're knowledgeable about allows you to generate revenue each time someone buys it, without the need for ongoing effort.

Further Example:
If you've learned how to create a profitable passive income strategy, you could write an eBook titled **"From Side Hustle to Passive Income: A Beginner's Guide"**. Platforms like **Amazon Kindle Direct Publishing (KDP)** allow you to publish and sell your eBook worldwide. Once published, it can continue to generate royalties as long as people keep buying it.

3. Printables and Templates

If you have design skills, creating printables or digital templates can be an excellent source of passive income. From planners to budgeting templates, people are always looking for ways to organize their lives more efficiently.

Further Example:
A simple idea could be a **planner template** for people looking to get organized in their business or personal finances. By selling it on platforms like **Etsy**, you can create a steady stream of income from each sale. These products can be sold in perpetuity once created.

B. Real Estate Investment

Real estate remains one of the most secure and reliable sources of passive income. While it may require a higher initial investment, the rewards—both short-term cash flow and long-term wealth building—are significant.

1. **Traditional Rental Properties**

Real estate is a time-tested method for generating passive income. By purchasing rental properties and leasing them to tenants, you can earn steady monthly income. Properties tend to appreciate over time, which can result in increased value and long-term wealth growth.

Further Example:
If you purchase a duplex or multi-family home and rent out the units, you can generate cash flow from rental income while the property's value appreciates over time. Renting out properties on **Airbnb** or **VRBO** can also yield higher returns, although it may require more active management.

2. **Real Estate Investment Trusts (REITs)**

If you don't want the hassle of managing physical properties, REITs provide an opportunity to invest in real estate without direct ownership. REITs pool funds from multiple investors to buy or manage real estate properties and offer shares that pay dividends.

Further Example:
If you have $5,000 to invest but aren't ready to purchase property outright, consider investing in a **REIT**. Companies like **Fundrise** or **RealtyMogul** allow investors to buy into real estate portfolios. REITs are an easy way to generate consistent dividends without the responsibility of being a landlord.

C. Stocks and Investments

1. **Dividend Stocks**

Dividend stocks are shares in companies that pay out a portion of their profits to shareholders on a regular basis. This is a great way to generate passive income without needing to sell your shares.

Further Example:
If you invest in a dividend-paying stock like **Coca-Cola**, you'll receive quarterly dividend payments, which can be

reinvested or used as income. As you acquire more dividend stocks over time, your income grows.

2. Peer-to-Peer Lending (P2P)

P2P lending involves lending money to individuals or businesses through online platforms in exchange for interest. It's an attractive option for people who want to earn higher returns than they might from traditional savings accounts or CDs.

Further Example:

Platforms like **LendingClub** allow you to lend money to borrowers for various purposes. If you lend $100 to a borrower at an interest rate of 8%, you'll earn interest payments over the loan's life. With the right risk management, P2P lending can provide high returns.

D. Content Creation

1. YouTube or Podcasting

Although it takes effort to create engaging content, YouTube and podcasting can be significant sources of passive income. Once you build a following, monetization can come from ad revenue, sponsorships, or affiliate marketing.

Further Example:

A YouTube channel focused on personal finance could generate revenue through ads and affiliate links to finance-related products, such as budgeting tools, investment apps, or credit cards.

2. Affiliate Marketing

Affiliate marketing involves promoting products or services through your blog, website, or social media platforms and earning a commission on each sale made through your affiliate links.

Further Example:

Suppose you run a fitness blog. You can include affiliate links to fitness gear, supplements, or workout programs in your posts. Each time a visitor clicks on your link and makes a purchase, you receive a commission.

3. Balancing High-Risk and Low-Risk Streams

As you diversify, it's essential to balance higher-risk passive income streams with more stable, low-risk options. High-risk streams can potentially generate higher returns but also come with the possibility of significant loss. Low-risk streams, on the other hand, tend to offer steady, reliable returns but with smaller growth potential.

Balancing Example:
If you're primarily focused on **dividend stocks** (a low-risk option), you might complement it with a **peer-to-peer lending portfolio** (a higher-risk option). This way, you can grow your passive income while protecting yourself from the volatility of any one stream.

4. Monitoring Your Passive Income Portfolio

Once you've diversified your income streams, it's crucial to monitor them to ensure you're optimizing each one. Regularly checking on the performance of your investments and other income sources will help you adjust your strategy when needed.

Key Metrics to Monitor:

- **ROI (Return on Investment):** How much profit you're generating compared to your initial investment.

- **Growth Rate:** Is your income increasing steadily, or is it flatlining?

- **Sustainability:** Is your income reliable, or are you depending on just one stream?

Adjusting Your Portfolio:
If a particular stream is underperforming or no longer aligns with your goals, it may be time to pivot or scale down. For

example, if your blog's affiliate sales are stagnant, you might want to update your content or change affiliate programs.

Conclusion of Chapter 6: Growing and Sustaining Your Income Portfolio

Diversifying your passive income portfolio is one of the smartest moves you can make to reduce risk, increase stability, and ensure long-term financial success. By incorporating various income streams—ranging from digital products and investments to real estate and content creation—you can create a robust system that works for you.

As you continue to expand your portfolio, remember that the key to sustained success is continuous learning, regular monitoring, and adapting to market changes.

5. Tools for Tracking and Optimizing Your Portfolio

In today's digital world, there are plenty of tools available to help you track, manage, and optimize your passive income portfolio. Whether you're managing real estate investments, stocks, digital products, or content creation, these tools can help you stay on top of performance and make informed decisions. Here are a few examples:

1. **Personal Finance Apps:**

Apps like **Mint** or **YNAB (You Need A Budget)** help you track income from various sources, set goals, and manage your finances. These tools can give you a clear overview of where your money is coming from and how much you're saving or reinvesting.

Example:
Using **Mint**, you can set up categories for different income streams, such as "real estate income," "dividends," and "ebook sales." This will give you a snapshot of how each

stream is performing, allowing you to make adjustments if needed.

2. Investment Platforms:

If you're involved in real estate investments or dividend stocks, platforms like **Fundrise**, **Robinhood**, or **M1 Finance** provide valuable insights into your investments, offering automated tracking and performance analysis.

Example:
On **Robinhood**, you can track the performance of your dividend stocks in real time, check dividend payout dates, and even reinvest those dividends automatically. This can help you maximize your returns without manually managing each transaction.

3. Google Analytics (for Digital Products):

If you are selling ebooks, online courses, or other digital products, using **Google Analytics** or **Shopify** analytics can help you track website traffic and sales. This allows you to optimize your sales strategies and see which products are performing the best.

Example:
By monitoring the data on your online course page, you can analyze how many people are signing up for the course, where they are coming from (organic search, social media, etc.), and what might be causing friction in the purchasing process.

4. Accounting Software:

Software like **QuickBooks** or **FreshBooks** helps you track income and expenses from various sources, create reports, and ensure that you are meeting tax obligations. As your passive income portfolio grows, these tools become essential for managing multiple streams.

Example:
If you have rental properties and also sell digital products, QuickBooks can help you track the income from both sources, categorize your expenses (property maintenance, advertising, etc.), and calculate net profit.

6. Scaling and Reinvesting for Growth

Once you've established multiple passive income streams and have begun diversifying, the next step is **scaling** your portfolio. This means expanding on successful streams, reinvesting your profits, and potentially adding new ventures to keep the growth momentum going.

Here are several strategies for scaling your passive income:

1. Reinvesting Profits into More Passive Income

One of the most powerful ways to scale your passive income portfolio is by reinvesting the profits you are earning. This could mean buying additional real estate properties, purchasing more dividend-paying stocks, or reinvesting in your content creation efforts (upgrading equipment, outsourcing, etc.).

Example:
Let us say you are making $500 per month from affiliate marketing. Instead of spending that money, you could reinvest it into paid advertising (Facebook ads, Google Ads) to drive more traffic to your website, which, in turn, could increase your affiliate sales.

2. Outsourcing to Scale Digital Products

If you are selling ebooks or courses, you might hit a point where you cannot keep up with demand or production. This is where outsourcing comes in. Hiring freelance writers, graphic designers, or video editors can free up your time and increase your ability to scale faster.

Example:
You have launched a successful ebook on passive income and now want to write more titles. Instead of doing everything yourself, you could hire a freelance writer to help produce additional content, or work with a designer to create accompanying workbooks and worksheets.

3. Leveraging Automation and Technology

To truly scale your passive income efforts, automation is key. Setting up systems to handle everything from payments and invoicing to email marketing and social media posting can save you time and increase efficiency.

Example:
If you are running an affiliate marketing blog, you can use tools like **MailChimp** or **ConvertKit** to automate email sequences that promote your affiliate products. These tools will send emails to your subscribers on autopilot, allowing you to promote products without manual effort.

4. Building Multiple Niche Websites or Blogs

If one website or blog is generating passive income, consider creating additional niche websites. This allows you to diversify your affiliate income and increase the potential for earnings.

Example:
If your blog on personal finance is doing well, you could create additional blogs targeting niches like **student loans**, **budgeting for families**, or **side hustle ideas**. Each blog would have its own set of affiliate links, creating multiple income streams.

7. Knowing When to Adjust or Exit

Even though passive income can be a long-term strategy, it's still important to regularly assess the performance of your portfolio. If a particular stream no longer aligns with your financial goals or is underperforming, it may be time to adjust or exit.

Signs it is Time to Exit or Adjust:

- **Stagnant Returns:** If a particular investment or income stream is not showing growth, it might be worth reassessing your strategy. For example, an online course that once sold well might need updates or a new marketing approach.

- **Emerging Opportunities:** Sometimes, new opportunities arise that can yield higher returns. If you discover a new, higher-yielding passive income stream, it might be wise to reallocate funds or efforts to capitalize on the new opportunity.

- **Changing Financial Goals:** As your financial situation changes, so might your goals. You may decide to shift from high-risk, high-reward strategies to more stable, long-term investments like dividend stocks or rental properties.

Example:
If your **real estate investments** are not yielding the returns you anticipated due to local market conditions, and you find that your **stock portfolio** is performing better, you may choose to sell one property and reinvest the proceeds into stocks. This kind of flexibility will help you optimize your portfolio's overall performance.

Practical Worksheets and Exercises

To help you implement the strategies discussed, here are a few worksheets and exercises:

Goal Setting Worksheet

- **What is your target passive income goal for the next year?**
- **What type of passive income stream do you want to start first?**
- **How many hours per week can you dedicate to your passive income journey?**

Financial Assessment Tool

- **How much capital do you currently have available to invest in passive income?**

- What are your current monthly expenses, and how much would you like your passive income to cover?

- What is your risk tolerance? Are you comfortable with investments that may require more time to yield returns?

Tracking Template

- Create a simple table to track your income sources and how much passive income each stream generates each month.

8. Conclusion: The Path to Long-Term Financial Freedom

In this chapter, we explored the importance of diversifying your passive income portfolio. The goal of diversification is to reduce risk, enhance stability, and create multiple streams of income that can grow over time.

By balancing high-risk, high-reward opportunities with stable, low-risk streams, and by regularly tracking, scaling, and adjusting your portfolio, you can build a financial future that offers long-term freedom. Whether you choose to expand your digital products, real estate investments, or other opportunities, the key to success is diversification, smart management, and reinvestment.

As you continue building your passive income empire, remember that it is not just about accumulating wealth—it is about creating a system that allows you the freedom to live life on your own terms.

This chapter provides you with a comprehensive understanding of how to diversify, manage, and scale your income sources effectively. The next chapter will focus on how to keep your passive income efforts sustainable for long-term financial success.

7 OVERCOMING CHALLENGES AND PITFALLS IN PASSIVE INCOME

While passive income is an attractive concept, the reality is that it often comes with its own set of challenges and pitfalls. Building a reliable income stream takes time, effort, and careful planning. In this chapter, we will explore some common obstacles that passive income earners face and how to overcome them. Understanding these challenges upfront can help you navigate them with greater ease and ensure that your passive income journey remains successful and sustainable.

1. Initial Investment and Upfront Effort

One of the most significant barriers to entering the passive income world is the **initial investment** required—whether in terms of time, money, or both. Many passive income streams, such as real estate or creating a high-quality online course, require significant upfront effort and sometimes capital.

Challenges:

- **Financial Investment:** To purchase rental properties, buy stocks, or start a business, you need a certain amount of capital to get started.

- **Time Investment:** Even with passive income streams, there is often considerable time required at the beginning. Writing an ebook, setting up an affiliate marketing website, or creating an online course can take weeks or even months.

How to Overcome:

- **Start Small and Scale:** You do not need a huge amount of capital to start. Begin with lower-cost passive income streams like digital products or affiliate marketing. Once you have learned the ropes and start seeing profits, you can scale up to higher-investment opportunities like real estate or larger businesses.

- **Budget and Plan:** If you are venturing into areas requiring significant financial investment, like real estate, create a solid budget and business plan. Look for ways to fund your investments, such as through savings, crowdfunding, or loans. Just be sure to understand your risk tolerance.

Example:
You might want to invest in a rental property but do not have enough capital to buy outright. In this case, you could start with **real estate crowdfunding platforms** like **Fundrise** or **RealtyMogul**, where you can invest in real estate projects for as little as $500. Over time, as you build your passive income from smaller investments, you can scale up.

2. Learning Curve and Knowledge Acquisition

Many passive income streams require learning new skills or understanding new industries. Whether it is real estate investing, digital marketing, or creating digital products, there is often a steep learning curve. This can be frustrating for new passive income earners who are eager to see returns quickly.

Challenges:

- **New Skills:** Writing, designing, or even understanding financial markets may not be second nature for you. Each passive income stream comes with a unique set of skills that you need to learn.

• **Research Time:** The time required to learn new systems and markets can be overwhelming, and without the proper knowledge, you might make costly mistakes.

How to Overcome:

• **Start with Education:** Before diving into a new passive income strategy, take time to learn. There are countless free and paid resources, including books, online courses, webinars, and blogs, that provide insights into various passive income strategies.

• **Leverage Mentorship and Communities:** Join communities or find mentors in the area you are interested in. Platforms like **Reddit**, **Facebook groups**, and **Discord** have communities for almost every niche, from blogging and e-commerce to real estate and investing.

Example:
If you are interested in starting a **real estate business**, consider taking a course on **BiggerPockets** or reading books like **"Rich Dad Poor Dad"** by Robert Kiyosaki. Connecting with experienced real estate investors on forums or in local meetups can give you invaluable insight into avoiding common pitfalls.

3. Cash Flow Volatility

While passive income can provide financial freedom, it's not always consistent. Some passive income streams, especially those based on investments, can experience periods of volatility, while others, like those in the digital products space, can be impacted by changing trends.

Challenges:

- **Seasonal Variations:** Some streams of passive income are seasonal, such as vacation rental properties or product sales during holiday seasons.

- **Market Fluctuations:** Stock market investments or other high-risk ventures can experience dips, affecting your overall cash flow.

How to Overcome:

- **Diversify Across Streams:** As we discussed in Chapter 6, diversifying your portfolio can buffer against volatility. Mix high-risk, high-reward ventures with low-risk, stable investments, like real estate or dividend stocks, to smooth out fluctuations.

- **Have Backup Cash Flow:** Create a "buffer" of savings that allows you to manage periods of lower passive income. This gives you the financial flexibility to weather lean months without dipping into your savings or relying on active income.

Example:
If you rely on Airbnb income, your cash flow might dip during the off-season. However, if you also have investments in **dividend stocks**, the steady quarterly payouts can provide a buffer during quieter months.

4. Maintenance and Ongoing Work

Despite the appeal of passive income, the truth is that some passive income streams still require **regular maintenance**. Whether it's ensuring your website remains optimized for SEO, updating an online course, or managing tenants in rental properties, passive income doesn't always mean "no work."

Challenges:

- **Ongoing Effort:** Some income streams require regular updates, troubleshooting, or occasional active involvement. For example, maintaining a blog for affiliate marketing success or monitoring your rental property's condition and tenants.

- **Keeping Up with Trends:** In rapidly changing markets (like digital products, social media, or investments), staying ahead of trends is crucial to maintaining a profitable income stream.

How to Overcome:

- **Automate Where Possible:** Automate processes like email marketing, product delivery, or social media posting to reduce the amount of active involvement you need.

- **Outsource Tasks:** As your income grows, consider outsourcing maintenance tasks to virtual assistants or freelancers. This allows you to focus on scaling your business without getting bogged down in day-to-day operations.

Example:
If you run a **blog** that generates income through affiliate marketing, automating email responses or scheduling social media posts with **tools like Buffer or Hootsuite** can help minimize time spent. Additionally, hiring a **content writer** or **SEO expert** can ensure your blog continues to rank highly without your constant involvement.

5. Legal and Tax Challenges

Navigating the legal and tax implications of passive income can be complicated, especially if you are managing multiple streams. Whether you are dealing with real estate, affiliate income, or digital products, understanding your tax obligations is crucial to avoid issues down the line.

Challenges:

- **Tax Complexity:** Different types of passive income are taxed differently, and the tax laws can vary by location and income level. Understanding capital gains, rental income, and self-employment taxes can be daunting.

- **Legal Obligations:** Owning rental properties, running a business, or selling digital products can require you to meet specific legal requirements (e.g., business licenses, taxes, insurance, etc.).

How to Overcome:

- **Consult a Professional:** It is often wise to consult with a tax advisor or accountant to ensure you're compliant with tax laws and maximizing your deductions.

- **Set Up a Legal Structure:** Consider setting up a legal structure for your business, such as an **LLC** (Limited Liability Company) or **S-Corp**, to protect yourself legally and streamline your tax filings.

Example:
If you're earning passive income from **renting out properties**, it's essential to understand tax deductions related to property management costs, depreciation, and repairs. A tax professional can help you optimize your tax strategy and avoid penalties.

6. Overcoming Fear and Self-Doubt

Lastly, many people face **self-doubt** when it comes to starting or growing their passive income ventures. Fear of failure, uncertainty about new strategies, or simply the overwhelming feeling of "I'm not sure if this will work" can hold you back.

Challenges:

- **Fear of Failure:** Starting something new can be intimidating, especially when you're putting in time or money and aren't sure what the results will be.

- **Overthinking:** Trying to perfect everything before starting can prevent you from ever getting started at all.

How to Overcome:

- **Take Small Steps:** Break down your goals into manageable steps. For example, instead of "launch a successful blog," start with "buy a domain name" or "write my first blog post." This helps to reduce the pressure and helps you take action.

- **Focus on Learning:** Remember that mistakes are part of the process. View them as opportunities to learn, rather than signs of failure. Every mistake teaches you something valuable for your future success.

Example:
If you are hesitant to start a **YouTube channel**, try creating a few practice videos and get feedback from friends or online communities. Once you gain confidence, you'll feel more comfortable diving in and monetizing your channel.

Conclusion: Persistence Pays Off

The road to creating and maintaining passive income is not always smooth, but it is incredibly rewarding. By understanding and overcoming the challenges discussed in this chapter, you can avoid common pitfalls and build a resilient passive income portfolio that grows and provides financial freedom.

Persistence, learning, and adapting to changing conditions are key to long-term success. Keep refining your approach, seeking knowledge, and making strategic decisions to scale and diversify your income streams. With the right mindset and approach, passive income will not just be a dream—it will be your reality.

Common Pitfalls and Mistakes to Avoid

Building passive income takes time, and many beginners make mistakes along the way. Here are some of the most common pitfalls:

Pitfall #1: Overestimating How Quickly You will See Results

Many people expect to start earning passive income immediately. However, the reality is that it often takes time to build and scale. Be prepared for a slow start and be patient with the process.

Pitfall #2: Failing to Diversify

Relying on just one income stream can be risky. If that stream falters or stops producing, you could be left with no income. Always aim to diversify across multiple sources.

Pitfall #3: Ignoring Taxes

Different forms of passive income are taxed differently. For example, rental income and dividends are subject to different tax rates. Make sure you understand the tax implications of your investments, and consult with a financial advisor to ensure you're optimizing your tax strategy.

Time Management and Productivity Tips

Creating passive income often requires consistent effort in the early stages. Here are some time management and productivity tips to help you balance your current job with your new ventures:

Tip #1: Block Time for Passive Income Work

Set aside specific blocks of time during your week for working on your passive income goals. Even 5–10 hours a week can make a significant difference over time.

Tip #2: Use Productivity Tools

Tools like Trello, Asana, or Notion can help you stay organized. You can create to-do lists, track progress, and set deadlines for each task associated with building your passive income.

Common Passive Income Tax Considerations

As you start generating passive income, it is important to understand how taxes impact your earnings. For example:

- **Rental Income:** This is taxed as regular income, but you can deduct expenses related to the property, such as repairs and property management fees.

- **Dividends and Interest:** These are typically taxed at a different rate than ordinary income, often at a lower rate.

- **Capital Gains:** When you sell an asset (like real estate or stocks) for a profit, you will pay capital gains taxes. The rate depends on how long you have held the asset.

Time vs. Money Tradeoff

Choosing the right passive income strategy depends largely on how much time and money you can invest upfront. The chart below compares common strategies based on these factors:

Strategy	Time Required (to Set Up)	Money Required (to Start)
Real Estate	Medium	High
Dividend Stocks	Low	Medium to High
Blogging	High	Low
Print-on-Demand	Medium	Low to Medium
Online Courses	Medium to High	Medium
Digital Products	Medium	Low

7. Conclusion: Persistence Pays Off

The road to creating and maintaining passive income is not always smooth, but it is incredibly rewarding. By understanding and overcoming the challenges discussed in this chapter, you can avoid common pitfalls and build a resilient passive income portfolio that grows and provides financial freedom.

Persistence, learning, and adapting to changing conditions are key to long-term success. Keep refining your approach, seeking knowledge, and making strategic decisions to scale and diversify your income streams. With the right mindset and approach, passive income will not just be a dream—it will be your reality.

Final Thoughts: Embrace the Journey

Building a portfolio of passive income requires patience and strategy. It is easy to get discouraged when things do not go as planned, or when early investments do not yield immediate results. However, success in passive income is often about playing the long game. The key is to stay adaptable, continuously learn, and diversify your streams of income. By doing so, you create a financial ecosystem that works for you, even when you are not actively working.

Remember, the challenges you face today are the learning experiences that will make you more capable tomorrow. Whether it is financial hurdles, technical difficulties, or self-doubt, know that each challenge you overcome is one step closer to the financial independence you seek.

By staying focused, continuing to refine your strategies, and expanding your knowledge, you will be well on your way to creating a sustainable and profitable passive income portfolio that can provide financial freedom for years to come.

In the next chapter, we will dive into the final steps to optimize your passive income and future-proof your financial independence for years ahead.

8 FUTURE-PROOFING YOUR PASSIVE INCOME PORTFOLIO

As you build and grow your passive income portfolio, it is important to consider not just the short-term gains, but also the long-term sustainability of your income streams. Future-proofing your passive income involves strategies to ensure that your financial freedom continues to grow and evolve over time, regardless of market changes or shifts in your personal circumstances. In this chapter, we will explore how to make your passive income strategies resilient, adaptable, and sustainable for years to come.

1. Diversification Across Asset Classes

One of the most powerful ways to future-proof your passive income portfolio is through **diversification**. Relying on just one income stream or asset class can expose you to significant risk if that market falters. By spreading your investments across various sectors, you reduce the likelihood of losing everything due to one setback.

Challenges:

- **Over-concentration in One Asset Class:** Relying too heavily on one type of passive income (e.g., rental properties, dividends, or affiliate marketing) can make your portfolio vulnerable to downturns in that particular area.

- **Volatility in Certain Markets:** High-growth markets like cryptocurrency or stock trading can be highly volatile and unpredictable.

How to Overcome:

- **Spread Your Investments:** Aim to build a diverse portfolio that includes a mix of real estate, dividend stocks, online businesses, digital products, and other alternative investments. This will help you smooth out the peaks and valleys that naturally occur in any one income stream.

- **Adapt to New Trends:** Stay aware of emerging trends and technologies that could provide new passive income opportunities. As industries evolve, your ability to pivot and include new income streams will help ensure your long-term success.

Example:
You could have rental properties generating steady income, a diversified stock portfolio providing dividend payments, a blog bringing in affiliate commissions, and an e-book offering royalty payments. This way, if one income stream faces a downturn (e.g., rental market slowdown), the others can help keep your overall income stable.

2. Automating and Outsourcing

To future-proof your passive income portfolio, consider **automation and outsourcing**. The beauty of passive income is that it should require minimal active involvement, but it often requires maintenance or updates. By automating many aspects of your income streams and outsourcing tasks, you free up more of your time for other pursuits while maintaining or even increasing your income.

Challenges:

- **Time Management:** Managing multiple income streams can become overwhelming if you're trying to keep everything running smoothly by yourself.

- **Increased Workload:** As your passive income grows, the amount of work needed to sustain it might grow as well. This can lead to burnout if you're not careful.

How to Overcome:

- **Use Technology:** Leverage automation tools to manage your online businesses. Use email marketing platforms, social media scheduling tools, and affiliate tracking software to automate repetitive tasks.

- **Outsource to Experts:** As your income grows, it's essential to delegate tasks like content creation, website management, customer support, or even bookkeeping to professionals. This allows you to focus on scaling your business or exploring new income opportunities.

Example:
For your blog or online business, consider using **Zapier** to automate social media posts or **Mailchimp** to automate email marketing. You can also hire a **virtual assistant** to handle customer inquiries or even a **freelancer** to write articles for your website, thus reducing your workload while still ensuring the business runs smoothly.

3. Stay Agile and Adapt to Changes

In today's rapidly evolving world, **flexibility** is key to future-proofing your passive income streams. Industries, technology, and consumer preferences change constantly, and what works today might not work tomorrow. Staying agile allows you to pivot when necessary and seize new opportunities as they arise.

Challenges:

- **Market Shifts:** The rise of new technologies, changing regulations, or shifting consumer habits can cause some passive income strategies to lose their effectiveness.

- **Stagnation:** Relying on outdated strategies or failing to evolve with trends can lead to missed opportunities and stagnation.

How to Overcome:

- **Continuous Learning:** Keep up with the latest trends in business, finance, and technology. Subscribe to industry blogs, take online courses, and attend conferences or webinars to stay ahead of the curve.

- **Experiment and Test:** Regularly test new strategies or investments. This could mean exploring new affiliate programs, launching a YouTube channel, or investing in emerging markets. Embrace change and be willing to evolve your portfolio as new opportunities arise.

Example:
If you have been relying on affiliate marketing through blog posts, consider diversifying into **YouTube** or **podcasting**—both growing platforms that could offer new streams of income. Additionally, you might explore **NFTs** or **cryptocurrency investments** if you have an interest in digital assets, as these markets are continually developing.

4. Reinvesting and Compounding

As you continue to earn passive income, one of the most powerful ways to future-proof your portfolio is to **reinvest your earnings**. Reinvesting your profits allows you to take advantage of **compounding**, where your money generates earnings on previous earnings, accelerating the growth of your wealth.

Challenges:

- **Spending the Profits:** It's tempting to spend the passive income you generate, especially if you're enjoying financial freedom. However, failing to reinvest can stunt the growth of your portfolio.

- **Slow Growth in Early Stages:** Passive income streams often grow slowly at first. It can take time to see significant returns, and many people get discouraged before their investments have had a chance to grow.

How to Overcome:

- **Commit to Reinvesting:** Develop a mindset where you consistently reinvest the majority of your earnings back into your portfolio. This could mean buying more assets, creating new content, or funding additional investments.

- **Track Your Progress:** Monitor your returns and the performance of your income streams so you can assess where reinvestment is most effective. Continuously fine-tune your approach to ensure maximum returns.

Example:
If you're earning passive income from a **stock portfolio**, consider reinvesting your dividends rather than cashing them out. Platforms like **Vanguard** and **Fidelity** offer options to automatically reinvest dividends, which can lead to exponential growth over time. Similarly, if you're earning royalties from **digital products**, you can reinvest those earnings into creating more products or expanding your marketing efforts.

5. Protecting Your Assets

To truly future-proof your passive income, you must also protect your assets. This includes financial protection, such as insurance or legal structures, and protecting your intellectual property and investments from unforeseen risks.

Challenges:

- **Risk of Loss:** As your passive income portfolio grows, so do the risks. Whether it's legal disputes, market downturns, or damage to physical assets (like rental properties), protecting your investments is crucial.

- **Asset Theft:** In the digital age, intellectual property theft or cyberattacks can be a real concern for online entrepreneurs and creators.

How to Overcome:

- **Insurance:** Consider **insurance** for your physical assets (e.g., rental properties) or even liability insurance for your business. This will protect you in the event of unforeseen issues.

- **Legal Protection:** Set up the right legal structures for your income streams. For example, an **LLC** or **S-Corp** can protect your personal assets in case of legal disputes related to your business.

- **Cybersecurity:** If your passive income involves digital products or online businesses, invest in cybersecurity measures, such as secure payment processing, website encryption, and data protection strategies.

Example:
If you are running a **digital product business**, make sure you have **copyrights** on your content and a **terms and conditions** agreement on your website to prevent unauthorized use of your material. Additionally, you can use **cybersecurity tools** like **Norton** or **Cloudflare** to protect your online business from hacking or data breaches.

6. Legacy and Succession Planning

Lastly, as you build your passive income portfolio, it is essential to think about **legacy planning**. Having a strategy in place for passing on your wealth ensures that the benefits of your hard work can continue for future generations.

Challenges:

- **Lack of Planning:** Many entrepreneurs fail to plan for the future, leaving their heirs to deal with the financial and legal complexities after they pass.

- **Transitioning the Business:** If your passive income involves a business, such as a blog or online store, you need to ensure that it can be seamlessly transferred to someone else, whether it's a family member or business partner.

How to Overcome:

- **Estate Planning:** Consult with an estate planner to set up a will, trusts, or other financial structures that allow your wealth to pass on smoothly.

- **Business Succession:** If your passive income is based on a business, ensure that you have a clear succession plan. This might involve training a successor or establishing a sale agreement for the business.

Example:
If you own a **real estate investment portfolio**, you might set up a **trust** to pass on the properties to your heirs, ensuring that they continue to generate passive income after your passing. Alternatively, for a **digital business**, you could create a plan to sell the business or pass it on to a family member.

Conclusion: Future-Proofing for Long-Term Success

Future-proofing your passive income portfolio requires a combination of diversification, automation, education, and legal protections. By thinking strategically and proactively managing risks, you can ensure that your passive income continues to grow and adapt as markets and technologies evolve.

7. Scaling Your Passive Income Streams

As you work to future-proof your portfolio, one of the most essential steps is to look for opportunities to **scale** your passive income streams. Scaling involves increasing the profitability of your existing income streams without proportionally increasing the time and effort you spend on them. By strategically scaling, you can increase your income while maintaining or even reducing the time commitment required to manage your portfolio.

Challenges:

- **Scaling Complexity:** As you scale your passive income streams, you may encounter complexities related to operations, management, and financing.

- **Risk of Overextension:** Growing your income streams too quickly or without sufficient planning can lead to burnout or mismanagement.

How to Overcome:

- **Automate Where Possible:** Use technology to your advantage. Tools that automate processes—such as marketing campaigns, payment systems, and customer service—can help you manage a larger volume of transactions without adding more work.

- **Outsource Strategically:** As you scale, it is important to hire experts or team members who can handle key tasks. For example, if you are scaling an online store, you might need to hire a logistics manager, digital marketers, or content creators to keep up with increased demand.

- **Focus on High-Return Areas:** Identify which of your passive income streams yield the highest returns and invest more resources into scaling those areas. This could involve increasing your portfolio of real estate properties, launching a new product, or expanding your digital marketing efforts.

Example:
If you have been earning passive income from **affiliate marketing** by writing a few blog posts, consider scaling by writing more content, diversifying into other platforms like YouTube or Instagram, or creating your own **digital product** to sell alongside affiliate offers. In real estate, scaling might mean using leverage (such as loans) to acquire additional properties, hiring a property manager, or automating rent collection.

8. Leveraging Debt and Credit Wisely

While many people view **debt** as something to avoid, when used wisely, **leverage** can be an effective tool for growing your passive income portfolio. Using other people's money (OPM) to finance investments allows you to increase the return on investment (ROI) without needing to put up the full capital yourself.

Challenges:

- **Risk of Over-Leverage:** Borrowing money to invest can lead to significant losses if the investments don't perform as expected. Poor management of debt can put you in financial jeopardy.

- **Interest and Fees:** Loans or credit often come with interest rates and fees that eat into your profits if not carefully managed.

How to Overcome:

- **Use Debt Cautiously:** Leverage should only be used in stable investments that are likely to provide a steady income stream. For example, using a mortgage to finance a rental property can be a good way to scale your real estate holdings without tying up all your personal savings.

- **Keep Debt Manageable:** Ensure that your debt repayments don't exceed the income generated by your passive income streams. One of the safest ways to use leverage is to ensure your monthly debt obligations are comfortably covered by your rental income, dividends, or other income sources.

- **Take Advantage of Low-Interest Credit:** Credit cards, home equity loans, or other forms of low-interest debt can provide funding for scaling your business or investments. However, always ensure the cost of financing is outweighed by the return you expect from the investment.

Example:
Using a **home equity loan** to buy additional rental properties can be an effective way to scale your real estate portfolio, as long as the rental income exceeds the loan payments. Alternatively, you could use a **business line of credit** to finance the creation and promotion of new digital products or online courses, increasing the reach of your business without putting your personal savings at risk.

9. Technology and Innovation: Staying Ahead of the Curve

To stay competitive and future-proof your income streams, embracing **technology and innovation** is essential. New tools, platforms, and business models are emerging all the time, and adopting the right technology can help you stay ahead of competitors, reduce costs, and increase your profits.

Challenges:

•   **Adapting to Rapid Change:** Technology evolves quickly, and it can be hard to keep up with the latest trends and tools.

•   **Investment Costs:** Adopting new technology often comes with an upfront cost or requires time to learn and implement.

How to Overcome:

•   **Stay Informed:** Regularly read industry blogs, attend webinars, and follow thought leaders to stay on top of new tools and technologies.

•   **Test New Technologies:** Do not be afraid to experiment with new software, platforms, or marketing techniques. Testing and adopting the right technologies early can give you a competitive edge in your niche.

•   **Be Selective:** Only invest in technologies that align with your passive income strategies. For example, if you are running an online business, tools like **Shopify** for e-commerce, **ClickFunnels** for sales funnels, and **Hootsuite** for social media management could significantly streamline your operations.

Example:
As the **AI** and **automation** space continues to evolve, consider integrating tools like **ChatGPT** for content creation or **Jasper AI** for social media posts, saving time and increasing efficiency in content marketing. Additionally, platforms like **Teachable** or **Udemy** can help you scale online courses, while **AI-powered tools** like **HubSpot** and **Zapier** can automate marketing and customer relationship management.

10. Building a Strong Network and Partnerships

Even though passive income is often about working independently, **building a strong network** and establishing **partnerships** can significantly enhance your opportunities and growth. Networking with like-minded individuals can expose you to new strategies, partnerships, and investment opportunities that you might not have discovered on your own.

Challenges:

- **Isolation:** Many passive income entrepreneurs work alone, and it can be easy to become isolated from others in the industry.

- **Finding the Right Partners:** Not every partnership or collaboration will be fruitful. It's important to align with individuals or organizations that share your values and goals.

How to Overcome:

- **Attend Networking Events:** Seek out conferences, online forums, and events related to passive income, investing, or entrepreneurship. These environments foster connections with people who can provide valuable insights or even joint ventures.

- **Leverage Online Communities:** Participate in online communities and social media groups, like **Reddit's personal finance forums**, **Facebook groups**, or **LinkedIn** to share ideas and collaborate on projects.

- **Form Strategic Partnerships:** Consider partnerships with influencers or other content creators who can help amplify your business or investment efforts. Joint ventures can significantly speed up growth when done correctly.

Example:
If you are running an online store, you might collaborate with an influencer to promote your products. Or, in real estate, teaming up with a fellow investor for joint ventures on larger properties can provide the capital and expertise needed to scale quickly.

Mindset and Motivation

Building passive income is not always easy, but it is worth the effort. Here are some mindset tips to stay on track:

- **Embrace Failure:** Failure is part of the process. Every failure provides valuable lessons that bring you closer to success.

- **Think Long-Term:** Passive income requires time to build. Do not get discouraged by short-term setbacks.

- **Stay Motivated:** Remember why you started. Whether it is for financial freedom, time flexibility, or the ability to pursue your passions, keep your end goals in mind.

Best Strategies by Audience

Below is a quick reference guide to help you identify passive income strategies best suited for your situation, based on your background, interests, and resources:

Audience	Recommended Strategies	Why

Students	Blogging, Print-on-Demand, Affiliate Marketing	Requires minimal capital, utilizes creativity
Professionals	Dividend Investing, Rental Properties, Online Courses	High scalability, uses expertise
Stay-at-Home Parents	Digital Products, Blogging, Printables	Flexible schedule, manageable from home
Retirees	Dividend Investing, REITs, Licensing Work	Reliable and low-effort income sources
Hobbyists and Creatives	Print-on-Demand, Stock Photos, Self-Publishing	Monetizes passions and skills
Tech-Savvy Individuals	SaaS, App Development, Website Themes	Leverages technical expertise for scalability

Conclusion: Future-Proofing Your Passive Income Portfolio for Lifelong Success

In this chapter, we have explored strategies to ensure that your passive income portfolio remains resilient and continues to grow for years to come. By diversifying, automating, leveraging technology, scaling wisely, and building strong networks, you can protect and expand your passive income streams in a way that allows you to enjoy financial freedom, even in the face of challenges.

As with any long-term financial strategy, the key to future-proofing is patience, persistence, and continual learning. By adopting the strategies discussed in this chapter, you are setting yourself up for a future of sustainable and growing wealth.

Next steps:
In the final chapter, we will summarize the key takeaways from the book and provide a roadmap to help you create your own passive income blueprint for success.

9 DEBUNKING MYTHS ABOUT PASSIVE INCOME

When people think of passive income, it is often shrouded in mystery and misconceptions. Popular media and online influencers frequently portray passive income as an effortless path to wealth, but the reality is far more nuanced. This chapter clears up some of the most common myths, providing you with a realistic foundation to pursue your passive income goals effectively.

Myth 1: Passive Income Requires No Work

One of the biggest misconceptions is that passive income streams require zero effort. While it is true that the goal is to minimize ongoing work, getting started usually demands significant time, energy, or financial investment.

Example:

- **Creating an online course** involves planning, recording, editing, and marketing.
- **Real estate investments** require research, maintenance, and tenant management.

Even after the setup phase, passive income streams may need periodic monitoring to ensure they stay profitable.

✓ **Callout Box: Pro Tip**
"The less work you want to put in later, the more effort you need to invest upfront."

Myth 2: You Need a Lot of Money to Start

The idea that passive income is only accessible to the wealthy is another common myth. While some strategies, like buying rental properties or investing in dividend stocks, do require substantial capital, there are plenty of low-cost options.

Examples of Low-Cost Passive Income Ideas:

- Starting a blog or YouTube channel.
- Selling digital products like eBooks or templates.

Quote Highlight:
"Creativity and time are often more valuable than financial resources when building passive income."

Myth 3: Passive Income is Quick and Easy

Many people believe passive income can replace their salary overnight. However, most strategies take time to build momentum.

Examples:

- **Blogs and YouTube channels** may take months or years to generate significant traffic and revenue.
- **Stock portfolios** need time to grow through compounding.

  ✓ **Callout Box: Real Talk**

"Patience and consistent effort are the secret ingredients to passive income success."

Myth 4: All Passive Income is Truly Passive

While the term "passive" suggests minimal involvement, many income streams require ongoing work.

Examples:

- **Rental properties** need occasional repairs, tenant screening, or management oversight.
- **Online courses** might need updates to remain relevant.

Tip: Automation tools can help reduce ongoing work, but regular engagement ensures long-term profitability.

Myth 5: Passive Income is Risk-Free

There's no such thing as a completely risk-free investment. Each passive income strategy has its own risks, such as:

- **Stocks:** Market volatility.
- **Real estate:** Economic downturns or local market conditions.
- **Online businesses:** Platform policy changes or increased competition.

✓ **Callout Box: Diversification Advice**
"Mitigating risk is all about diversification. Do not put all your eggs in one basket."

Myth 6: Passive Income Will Replace Your Salary Immediately

Building a passive income stream that fully replaces your active income takes time and dedication.

Reality: It is more realistic to treat passive income as a supplement to your salary in the beginning. Over time, your income streams may grow to provide financial independence.

Myth 7: Only Experts Can Build Passive Income

Many believe that passive income requires specialized knowledge or expertise.

Reality: Most passive income strategies are accessible to beginners. Platforms like Canva, Teachable, and Amazon KDP simplify the process of creating and selling digital products.

> ✓ **Callout Box: Encouragement**
> *"You don't need to be an expert to start—learning as you go is part of the journey."*

Myth 8: Passive Income is a "Set and Forget" System

The notion that passive income streams require zero ongoing effort is misleading. Most streams need periodic maintenance, such as:

- Updating content for blogs or courses.
- Monitoring investment portfolios.
- Engaging with audiences for platforms like YouTube or social media.

Quote Highlight:
"Passive income isn't about no work; it's about smart work."

Engaging Stories

Sarah's Blogging Journey

Sarah started a blog about personal finance with no prior experience. She spent months writing articles, building an audience, and learning SEO. For over a year, her income was minimal—less than $100 per month. But by year three, her blog was generating $10,000 per month through affiliate marketing and ads.

- ✓ **Lesson:** Consistent effort pays off in the long run.

James' Print-on-Demand Success

James worked full-time but wanted extra income. He started a print-on-demand T-shirt shop on Etsy. Initially, he lacked design skills, so he learned Canva and experimented. Within two years, his shop grew steadily, earning $4,000 per month.

- ✓ **Lesson:** Start small and improve your skills as you grow.

Conclusion: Myth-Busting for Success

Dispelling these myths is essential for setting realistic expectations and building sustainable income streams. Passive income isn't a magic formula—it's a combination of upfront effort, patience, and continuous learning. But the rewards, including financial freedom and security, are worth the journey.

Final Thought:
"With realistic expectations and a willingness to adapt, passive income can become your most reliable path to long-term financial independence."

10 Overcoming Challenges on Your Passive Income Journey

Embarking on the path to passive income and financial freedom is an exciting endeavor, but it is not without its challenges. While the idea of earning money with minimal effort is appealing, the reality requires persistence, adaptability, and a proactive approach to problem-solving. In this chapter, we will explore common challenges you may face and provide strategies to overcome them.

1. Challenge: Finding the Right Opportunity

Obstacle: With countless passive income ideas out there, it can feel overwhelming to choose the right one for your goals and skills.
Solution:

- **Self-assessment:** Reflect on your strengths, interests, and available resources. For instance, if you enjoy writing, creating e-books or blogs may suit you. If you have capital to invest, real estate or dividend stocks might be a better fit.

- **Start small:** Test one idea with minimal investment to see how it works before committing fully.

2. Challenge: Initial Time and Effort

Obstacle: Building a passive income stream often requires significant upfront effort, such as creating a digital product or setting up a rental property.
Solution:

•   **Set realistic expectations:** Understand that passive income is rarely instant. It is an investment of time and energy upfront for long-term rewards.

•   **Break it down:** Divide large tasks into smaller, manageable steps to make progress without feeling overwhelmed.

3. Challenge: Financial Barriers

Obstacle: Many passive income opportunities require initial capital, which can be a barrier for beginners.
Solution:

•   **Low-cost options:** Explore affordable passive income ideas, like print-on-demand products, affiliate marketing, or creating low-cost e-books.

•   **Reinvest profits:** Use earnings from one income stream to fund other ventures, gradually expanding your portfolio.

4. Challenge: Market Competition

Obstacle: Certain passive income opportunities, like online courses or real estate, may have high competition.
Solution:

•   **Niche down:** Identify underserved niches within your chosen field. For example, instead of a general fitness blog, focus on "fitness for busy professionals."

•   **Differentiate:** Offer unique value, such as superior customer service, innovative ideas, or a personal touch that sets you apart.

5. Challenge: Maintaining Motivation

Obstacle: The delayed gratification of passive income can test your patience and determination.

Solution:

- **Celebrate small wins:** Acknowledge progress, even if it's just publishing your first blog post or earning your first dollar.

- **Visualize your goals:** Remind yourself why you started. Picture the freedom and opportunities passive income will provide.

6. Challenge: Navigating Failures

Obstacle: Not every idea will succeed, and setbacks are inevitable.
Solution:

- **Embrace failure as a teacher:** Learn from what didn't work and use those lessons to improve future ventures.

- **Diversify:** Avoid putting all your efforts into one project. By spreading your focus across multiple streams, you reduce risk and increase your chances of success.

7. Challenge: Staying Adaptable

Obstacle: Markets and technologies change, which can affect your income streams.
Solution:

- **Stay informed:** Regularly educate yourself on trends and updates in your industry.

- **Be flexible:** Be ready to pivot or evolve your strategies when necessary. For example, if one platform becomes less effective, explore new avenues.

Final Thoughts:

Overcoming challenges is part of the journey to achieving financial freedom. Every obstacle you face and conquer is a stepping stone toward building resilience and long-term success. Remember, persistence and adaptability are your greatest allies. Embrace the process, stay focused on your goals, and trust that your efforts will pay off in the form of financial independence and a fulfilling life.

11 Passive Income and Financial Freedom

In this chapter, we will explore the relationship between passive income and achieving financial freedom. The pursuit of financial freedom is a goal for many, and passive income plays a central role in that journey. By building reliable passive income streams, you can create the financial independence that allows you to live life on your own terms.

What is Financial Freedom?

Financial freedom means having enough income from your investments, assets, or business ventures that you no longer rely on your job to cover your living expenses. It allows you to make choices based on what you want, rather than what you need. Financial freedom gives you the power to:

•	**Spend your time as you choose**, whether that's pursuing hobbies, traveling, or spending more time with family.

•	**Live debt-free**, which offers peace of mind and the ability to save and invest more for the future.

•	**Retire early**, or transition to part-time work, giving you flexibility and control over your career.

•	**Increase your wealth** over time through smart investments and growing your passive income streams.

How Passive Income Leads to Financial Freedom

Passive income provides the foundation for financial freedom by generating income without requiring constant work. Unlike earned income, which comes from your job, passive income works for you, creating a sustainable flow of cash that can cover your expenses and support your lifestyle. Here's how passive income helps:

- **Earnings without constant effort:** Once a passive income stream is set up, it continues to generate income with little ongoing work.

- **Scalability:** Many passive income sources, like digital products, online businesses, or real estate investments, can be scaled to increase earnings.

- **Reduced reliance on active income:** As your passive income grows, you become less dependent on your job and can allocate more time to pursuits you enjoy.

Types of Passive Income That Promote Financial Freedom

Different types of passive income allow you to create financial freedom in various ways. Some sources require more initial effort or capital investment, while others are more accessible to beginners. Let us explore some of the top passive income streams that can help you build financial independence:

1. Real Estate Investing

Real estate is one of the most well-known paths to financial freedom. By investing in rental properties, you can generate consistent rental income while building equity over time. Key ways to benefit from real estate include:

- **Rental Properties:** Owning single-family homes, multi-family units, or commercial properties can generate steady cash flow, especially in high-demand areas.

- **Real Estate Investment Trusts (REITs):** If you don't want the responsibility of managing physical properties, you can invest in REITs, which pool funds from many investors to buy and manage real estate assets.

Real-Life Example:
Tom and Jane invested in rental properties in 2010. By 2020, their properties were fully paid off, and their rental income provided a consistent flow of $5,000 per month, covering all their living expenses and more. With their rental income, they were able to retire early and travel the world.

2. Dividend Stocks and Investments

Investing in dividend-paying stocks or funds is another excellent way to generate passive income. Dividends are regular payments made by companies to shareholders, often quarterly. By investing in high-quality dividend stocks or mutual funds, you can create a steady stream of income over time.

- **Blue-chip stocks:** Companies with strong track records of paying dividends, such as Coca-Cola, Apple, and Procter & Gamble, are popular choices.

- **Dividend reinvestment plans (DRIPs):** These plans allow you to automatically reinvest dividends to buy more shares, compounding your earnings over time.

Real-Life Example:
Sarah invested $100,000 in a diversified dividend stock portfolio. After a few years, her annual dividend income reached $6,000, which grew each year as she reinvested the dividends. By the time she reached 50, the dividends covered her entire living expenses.

3. Digital Products

Creating and selling digital products, such as eBooks, courses, stock photos, printables, or software, is a powerful way to generate passive income. Once created, these products can be sold continuously with little to no extra work.

- **Online Courses:** If you have expertise in a niche area, you can create and sell an online course through platforms like Teachable or Udemy.

- **eBooks and Guides:** Writing eBooks or guides and selling them through Amazon KDP or your website can generate long-term income with little additional work once published.

Real-Life Example:

John wrote an eBook about personal finance, which he sold through Amazon KDP. Initially, it did not sell well, but after a few months of consistent marketing, sales picked up, and it generated around $2,000 per month. After two years, the book became a reliable income stream, giving him the ability to quit his job and focus on other entrepreneurial ventures.

4. Peer-to-Peer Lending and Crowdfunding

Peer-to-peer (P2P) lending allows you to lend money to individuals or small businesses in exchange for interest payments. Crowdfunding platforms, like Fundrise, allow you to invest in real estate projects with relatively low capital requirements.

- **P2P Lending:** Platforms like LendingClub and Prosper allow you to loan money directly to individuals or small businesses, earning interest on your investment.

- **Real Estate Crowdfunding:** Fundrise and RealtyMogul enable you to invest in real estate projects with smaller amounts of capital, receiving passive returns from the property's rental income or eventual sale.

Real-Life Example:
Michael invested $10,000 into a real estate crowdfunding project. Over the next three years, the project generated a 12% return, earning him $1,200 annually without any involvement in the management of the property.

5. Creating an Online Business

Building an online business, whether it's an eCommerce store, a dropshipping venture, or a subscription-based service, can lead to significant passive income once the processes are automated.

- **eCommerce & Dropshipping:** Selling physical products through platforms like Shopify or Amazon can create passive income through automated fulfillment systems.

- **Affiliate Marketing:** Promoting other companies' products on your blog, YouTube channel, or social media and earning commissions from sales is a great way to generate passive income.

Real-Life Example:
Rachel started an online store selling handmade jewelry. After automating her inventory and outsourcing customer service, her business generated steady passive income while she focused on marketing and product development.

6. Licensing and Royalties

Licensing your intellectual property—whether it's music, photography, art, or even patents—can create recurring passive income. Artists, photographers, and inventors can license their work to be used in films, commercials, websites, and more.

- **Music Royalties:** If you compose music, you can earn royalties every time it's played on the radio, in movies, or in commercials.

- **Photographs and Artwork:** By licensing your work on platforms like Shutterstock or Adobe Stock, you can earn royalties each time your image is downloaded.

Real-Life Example:
Chris, a photographer, began uploading his photos to stock photography websites. Over the years, he built a portfolio of 500+ images, and today his monthly royalty income covers his living expenses, allowing him to focus on other creative projects.

Here are some additional tips and resources you can include to make Chapter 10 even more actionable for your readers:

Additional Tips for Building Passive Income Toward Financial Freedom

While the passive income strategies discussed in this chapter are powerful tools, it's important to keep in mind that success doesn't happen overnight. Here are some essential tips to help you on your journey toward financial freedom:

1. Start Small, Scale Gradually

Building passive income requires time, patience, and a clear strategy. Rather than diving into a large project right away, start small and test the waters. For example, you can begin by creating a single online course or publishing an eBook before branching out into other income streams. This allows you to learn from your mistakes without risking too much capital upfront.

Tip:

"Start with one project, master it, and once it's running smoothly, scale it up or diversify into another stream."

2. Reinvest Your Earnings

Reinvesting your passive income is key to growing your wealth over time. Whether it's reinvesting dividends, profits from your digital products, or rental income, putting your earnings back into your investments allows them to compound and generate more income in the future.

Example:
If you earn $100 per month from a digital product, reinvest it into marketing or creating new products. This will help you increase your earnings and grow your passive income empire.

3. Diversify Your Income Streams

While it's tempting to focus on just one source of passive income, diversifying across several streams reduces risk and ensures more stability in your financial future. By combining real estate, stocks, digital products, and more, you're not reliant on any one source.

Tip:
"Don't put all your eggs in one basket—spread your investments and income streams to protect yourself from market volatility or unforeseen changes."

4. Automate as Much as Possible

Automation is one of the most effective ways to reduce the amount of work required to maintain passive income streams. Use tools and software to automate tasks like email marketing, social media posting, or inventory management for your eCommerce store. Automation allows you to focus on scaling your business rather than day-to-day operations.

Tool Recommendations:

- **Email Marketing Automation:** ConvertKit, MailChimp
- **Ecommerce Automation:** Shopify, WooCommerce
- **Social Media Scheduling:** Buffer, Hootsuite

5. Keep Learning and Adapting

The world of passive income is dynamic. New tools, platforms, and opportunities are constantly emerging. Keep up-to-date with the latest trends and innovations in passive income by reading blogs, joining online communities, and attending webinars or workshops.

Resources:

- **Podcasts:**
  - *The Side Hustle School*
  - *Smart Passive Income Podcast*
  - *The Financial Independence Podcast*
- **Books:**
  - *The 4-Hour Workweek* by Tim Ferriss
  - *Rich Dad Poor Dad* by Robert Kiyosaki
  - *The Millionaire Fastlane* by MJ DeMarco

Practical Resources for Passive Income

Here are some practical resources to help you get started with the passive income strategies mentioned earlier:

1. Real Estate Platforms

- **Fundrise**: A real estate crowdfunding platform that lets you invest in real estate projects for as little as $500.

- **Roofstock**: A marketplace for buying and selling single-family rental properties that already have tenants.

- **Airbnb**: If you own a property or have a spare room, renting it out on Airbnb can generate substantial passive income.

2. Online Course Platforms

- **Teachable**: A popular platform for creating and selling online courses.

- **Udemy**: A marketplace where you can upload and sell courses to a broad audience.

- **Skillshare**: Allows creators to earn passive income by uploading educational content.

3. Investment Platforms

- **Acorns**: A micro-investing app that rounds up your purchases and invests the spare change into a diversified portfolio.

- **Betterment**: A robo-advisor that automates investments to help you grow your wealth over time.

- **Vanguard**: Offers low-cost, passive index funds ideal for building a long-term portfolio.

4. Digital Product Tools

- **Canva**: Create and sell digital products such as printables, planners, or artwork.

- **Etsy**: A platform where you can sell your digital creations like art prints, templates, and stationery.

- **Amazon KDP**: Self-publish eBooks and paperbacks and earn royalties with minimal ongoing effort.

5. Peer-to-Peer Lending Platforms

- **LendingClub**: Lend money to individuals or small businesses, earning interest on your investment.

- **Prosper**: A peer-to-peer lending platform that allows you to invest in personal loans.

Conclusion: Your Path to Financial Freedom

Achieving financial freedom through passive income isn't about finding a shortcut—it's about making smart, consistent efforts over time. With the right mindset, dedication, and a willingness to learn, you can build multiple income streams that will provide the financial independence you desire.

Remember, the journey to financial freedom may take time, but the rewards are worth the effort. Stay focused, reinvest your profits, and always be on the lookout for new opportunities. Whether you want to retire early, quit your day job, or simply gain more control over your time, passive income can help you get there.

Final Thought:
"Financial freedom isn't just about the money—it's about the freedom to live life the way you've always dreamed."

These tips and resources are designed to help readers take actionable steps toward creating lasting passive income streams. Let me know if you need more examples or adjustments!

12 Creating Your Personalized Income Blueprint

Now that you have learned about the various types of passive income streams and strategies to future-proof your portfolio, it is time to put it all together. In this final chapter, we'll guide you through the process of creating your own personalized **passive income blueprint**. This blueprint will act as your roadmap to achieving financial independence, ensuring that you have a step-by-step plan that suits your lifestyle, risk tolerance, and financial goals.

By the end of this chapter, you will be equipped with a solid framework to take action and start building, optimizing, and growing your passive income portfolio.

1. Define Your Financial Goals and Timeline

Before diving into any income stream, it's essential to establish clear **financial goals**. What does financial independence look like for you? Are you looking for a few hundred extra dollars a month, or do you want to generate enough passive income to replace your full-time job?

Key Questions to Ask:

- What is your target monthly passive income goal?

- Do you want to quit your 9-to-5 job, or are you building additional income streams to supplement your current income?

- **What timeline are you working with?** Are you looking for short-term results, or are you aiming for long-term wealth accumulation?

Setting these goals is crucial because they will determine the types of passive income streams you pursue and how much time and capital you invest in them. If you're aiming for financial freedom in five years, you'll likely want to focus on income streams with a faster growth trajectory. On the other hand, if your goal is long-term wealth-building, you may focus on more stable and low-maintenance investments.

Example:
If your goal is to replace your full-time job income with passive income in three years, you may prioritize scalable digital products like online courses or affiliate marketing. However, if you're aiming to retire comfortably in 20 years, you might lean towards real estate investing and dividend stocks for long-term growth.

2. Assess Your Starting Point

Before you embark on any passive income strategy, it's essential to assess your **current financial situation**. Understanding where you stand financially will help you determine what type of investment and income streams you can start with and how much capital or time you have to dedicate.

Key Questions to Ask:

- **How much capital do you have to invest?** (e.g., savings, investment capital)

- **How much time can you commit to learning and managing passive income sources?**

- **What is your risk tolerance?** Are you comfortable with more volatile investments, or do you prefer stability?

How to Proceed:

- **Create a Budget:** Take a look at your income and expenses to determine how much money you can invest or reinvest into your passive income streams. For example, if you have a stable job, you can afford to dedicate a portion of your income to investing in real estate or stocks.

- **Time Commitment:** Decide how much time you're willing to invest in learning new skills or managing your investments. Some passive income streams, like affiliate marketing or real estate, require an initial time investment to set up. Others, like dividend stocks or automated businesses, may require less active management.

- **Risk Assessment:** If you're risk-averse, you may prefer income streams that are low-risk, such as dividend-paying stocks or high-yield savings accounts. If you're open to higher risk, you might consider cryptocurrency investments or high-growth digital products.

3. Select Your Passive Income Streams

Now that you have a clear understanding of your goals and starting point, it's time to decide which **passive income streams** you want to focus on. In this chapter, we've covered a wide variety of options, including real estate, stocks, online businesses, and more. The key is to choose income streams that align with your financial goals, time commitment, and risk tolerance.

Example of a Balanced Portfolio:

- **Real Estate:** A few rental properties to generate steady monthly income.

- **Dividend Stocks:** Low-maintenance investments that pay regular dividends.

- **Online Business:** A blog or YouTube channel for affiliate marketing or ad revenue.

- **Digital Products:** E-books, courses, or printables to create scalable income.

- **Peer-to-Peer Lending:** Invest in loans to earn interest over time.

Action Step:
Select one or two passive income streams to start with. It's essential to focus your energy and resources on mastering a few streams before expanding into others.

4. Develop a Step-by-Step Action Plan

Now that you've selected your income streams, it's time to create a **step-by-step action plan**. This plan should break down each income stream into manageable tasks and set clear milestones along the way. Having a clear plan will help you stay on track and measure your progress over time.

Example Action Plan for Real Estate Investment:

- **Step 1:** Research local real estate markets to identify high-potential properties.

- **Step 2:** Secure financing and obtain pre-approval for a mortgage.

- **Step 3:** Find a property, negotiate the price, and finalize the purchase.

- **Step 4:** Hire a property manager or set up a system for managing tenants.

- **Step 5:** Begin collecting rent and reinvest the profits into additional properties.

For online businesses or digital products:

- **Step 1:** Research profitable niches for your blog, YouTube channel, or e-commerce store.

- **Step 2:** Create content or a product to sell (e.g., a course, e-book, or printables).

- **Step 3:** Set up your website and marketing funnels (e.g., email marketing, social media, or paid ads).

- **Step 4:** Optimize for traffic and conversions (SEO, A/B testing, etc.).

- **Step 5:** Scale by adding more content, expanding product lines, or automating your marketing.

5. Monitor, Adjust, and Optimize

Your passive income blueprint isn't static. As you progress, it's important to continuously **monitor**, **adjust**, and **optimize** your portfolio to ensure it's working as effectively as possible. Regularly evaluate your income streams, look for opportunities to improve them, and make adjustments when necessary.

Key Questions to Ask:

- Are your passive income streams generating the expected results?

- What strategies or tactics have been the most successful?

- Do you need to shift your focus to new opportunities or markets?

How to Proceed:

- **Track Your Progress:** Use tools like spreadsheets, financial tracking apps, or portfolio management software to track your income from each source. Regularly review your goals and compare them with actual results.

- **Adjust Your Strategy:** If you find that one income stream is underperforming, don't be afraid to pivot or try new strategies. For example, if affiliate marketing isn't generating the returns you expected, you might consider diversifying into creating digital products or running paid ads.

- **Reinvest Earnings:** As your income grows, consider reinvesting profits into more scalable opportunities, such as expanding your real estate portfolio or developing additional digital products.

Example:
You might start by focusing on dividend stocks and real estate. As your income from these streams grows, you could use the profits to invest in an online business or create a digital product, such as an e-book, that generates automated income.

6. Stay Committed and Patient

Creating a passive income portfolio takes time, effort, and patience. While it may be tempting to focus only on the quick wins, remember that passive income is often a long-term strategy. By staying committed to your blueprint and continuously learning, you'll gradually build a sustainable portfolio that provides financial freedom.

Remember:

- **Patience is Key:** Passive income typically takes time to build. Real estate requires capital, online businesses require time to grow, and investments need time to compound. Be patient and don't expect instant results.

- **Continuous Learning:** Keep educating yourself about the strategies you're implementing. Attend workshops, read books, and connect with other passive income enthusiasts to gain new insights.

- **Enjoy the Journey:** While the goal is financial independence, don't forget to enjoy the process. Celebrate small wins, and remember that each step brings you closer to your ultimate goal of financial freedom.

Case Studies and Real-Life Examples

Example 1: Sarah's Real Estate Journey

Sarah, a 35-year-old teacher, was tired of living paycheck to paycheck. She started her passive income journey by researching real estate investing. After saving for a down payment on a small rental property, she bought a duplex. The monthly rental income from the second unit covered her mortgage, making her home essentially free. Over time, she acquired additional properties, and now, at age 40, Sarah generates enough passive income to cover all her living expenses, allowing her to work part-time or even pursue her passion projects.

Example 2: Tom's Online Business Success

Tom, a 28-year-old software engineer, started a blog about personal finance while working full-time. Initially, it was a hobby, but after a year, he began monetizing it through affiliate marketing and selling his own e-books. Over the next three years, his income grew to over $10,000 a month, and now, Tom has fully transitioned into running his online business, which provides him with a comfortable passive income that allows him to travel the world.

Conclusion: Your Path to Financial Freedom

By following the steps outlined in this chapter, you now have a **personalized passive income blueprint** tailored to your unique financial goals, starting point, and preferences. Remember that building passive income is a journey, not a race. Each income stream you create and optimize will bring you closer to financial freedom, and with the right strategy, commitment, and patience, you can build a portfolio that supports the lifestyle you desire.

With your blueprint in hand, it is time to take action. Start small, focus on one income stream at a time, and remember that the path to financial independence is a marathon, not a sprint.

13 Mastering Patience and Persistence

Building passive income is like planting a garden: you sow seeds today with the expectation of enjoying a flourishing harvest in the future. However, just as gardens require consistent care, patience, and time, so do passive income streams. This chapter dives into the critical skills of patience and persistence, which are indispensable for long-term success.

The Long Game of Passive Income

Passive income is not a get-rich-quick scheme—it is a long-term strategy for financial independence. Many people abandon their efforts prematurely because they do not see immediate results. Understanding the nature of compounding growth and delayed gratification is key.

Case Study: The Power of Compounding
Imagine investing $100 a month into a dividend stock portfolio that yields 8% annually. In 10 years, you would have contributed $12,000, but with compounding, your portfolio would be worth over $18,000. The longer you wait, the greater the growth. By year 20, it could be worth over $60,000. Small, consistent actions can lead to exponential rewards over time.

Dealing with Delayed Results

Most passive income streams require significant upfront effort before yielding returns. Here's how to stay focused:

1. **Set Milestones:** Break down your long-term goal into smaller, achievable steps.

- Example: If you're writing an e-book, aim to complete one chapter per week.

2. **Track Your Progress:** Use tools or journals to monitor your efforts and small wins.

- Example: If you're starting a blog, track website traffic growth month by month.

3. **Visualize the Outcome:** Remind yourself of the freedom and opportunities passive income will provide in the future.

Overcoming Challenges

It's common to feel discouraged during the initial stages. Here's how to overcome common obstacles:

1. Lack of Motivation

- **Solution:** Connect with a support system or community of like-minded individuals. Join forums, attend webinars, or participate in mastermind groups to stay inspired.

2. Financial Constraints

- **Solution:** Focus on methods that require low or no upfront investment, such as affiliate marketing, blogging, or selling digital products. Gradually reinvest profits to grow your efforts.

3. Fear of Failure

- **Solution:** Reframe failure as a learning opportunity. Analyze what didn't work, make adjustments, and move forward. Every successful entrepreneur has faced setbacks but persisted through them.

The Role of Consistency

Persistence is not just about working hard—it's about working smart, regularly, and sustainably.

•   **Example:** If you're investing in stocks, automate monthly contributions to ensure consistency without requiring ongoing decision-making.

•   **Example:** If you're building an audience, commit to posting one high-quality blog post or video each week.

Even modest but regular efforts can lead to substantial results over time.

Motivation from Success Stories

Hearing about others' journeys can be a powerful motivator. Consider the story of Sarah, who started selling handmade jewelry on Etsy. At first, she earned just $50 a month. Through persistence and consistent effort, she expanded her product range and optimized her listings. Five years later, she now generates $5,000 a month in largely passive income.

Practical Exercises to Build Persistence

1. Create a "Why" Statement:
Write down why you want to build passive income and what it will allow you to achieve. Keep this visible as a reminder of your purpose.

2. Practice Time Blocking:
Dedicate specific blocks of time to work on your passive income projects. Consistent effort, even in short bursts, leads to progress.

3. Reward Yourself:

Celebrate small milestones. Completed your first e-book? Treat yourself to a nice dinner. Reached $1,000 in monthly passive income? Take a weekend getaway.

The Ripple Effect of Patience

When you stay the course, your efforts have a ripple effect. What starts as a small stream of income can grow into a river over time. Your patience and persistence will not only lead to financial rewards but also develop invaluable habits of discipline, resilience, and forward-thinking.

Key Takeaways

- Passive income requires consistent effort and the ability to embrace delayed gratification.

- Set clear milestones, track progress, and stay motivated with small wins.

- Persistence is the key to overcoming challenges and achieving exponential growth.

By mastering patience and persistence, you set yourself apart from those who give up too soon. Your journey may take time, but the rewards will be worth it. Remember, the seeds you plant today will bear fruit tomorrow.

Community Building and Networking

One of the most powerful ways to accelerate your passive income growth is by networking and collaborating with others who share your goals. You can find communities through:

- **Online forums** like BiggerPockets for real estate investors or Reddit's passive income threads.
- **Mastermind groups** that allow you to brainstorm and share strategies with others.
- **Social media groups** for affiliate marketers, content creators, or investors.

Next Steps:

In the final section, we will revisit some of the most important concepts from the book and offer final thoughts to inspire you on your passive income journey.

Good luck on your journey toward financial freedom!

Final Thoughts: Embracing the Journey to Financial Freedom

As you have learned throughout this book, building a successful passive income portfolio is not about taking shortcuts or seeking instant riches. It is about creating a sustainable strategy that aligns with your goals, values, and resources. Passive income is not a get-rich-quick scheme; rather, it is a gradual and deliberate process of creating multiple streams of income that work for you even when you are not actively working.

A Roadmap or Timeline for Passive Income Success

Here is a simple timeline to guide your journey toward passive income:

1. **Month 1–3: Research and Education**

   • Spend time understanding different income streams and choose one to start with.

   • Begin building your first passive income source (real estate, online business, etc.).

2. **Month 4–6: Implement and Track Progress**

   • Launch your first passive income project. Track your progress and make adjustments where necessary.

3. **Month 7–12: Scale and Diversify**

    • Once you have a successful stream, consider scaling it or adding a second income source. Diversify across different models for greater security.

4. **Year 2 and Beyond: Optimize and Automate**

    • Automate your processes and start seeing true passive income results. Use your profits to reinvest in more lucrative opportunities.

Key Takeaways:

1. **Start Small, Scale Gradually:** Begin with one or two passive income streams, and once they are generating consistent income, look for opportunities to scale. Do not try to do everything at once—focus your efforts and expand as you gain experience and confidence.

2. **Diversification is Critical:** Do not put all your eggs in one basket. Diversify your portfolio across different types of passive income streams—real estate, stocks, digital products, and more—to minimize risk and maximize opportunities for growth.

3. **Reinvest and Optimize:** Use the income you generate to reinvest in your business or portfolio. Whether it is buying more properties, launching a new product, or investing in more stocks, reinvesting profits is a powerful tool to accelerate growth.

4. **Stay Educated and Adaptable:** The world of passive income is constantly evolving, with new tools, platforms, and strategies emerging regularly. Keep learning, stay up-to-date, and be willing to adapt your approach as necessary to stay ahead of the curve.

5. **Patience is Key:** Success in passive income does not happen overnight. You will need to put in the work upfront, but the rewards—financial freedom, time flexibility, and peace of mind—are well worth the effort. Stay patient and committed to the process, and you will see the fruits of your labor.

Your Next Steps:

Now that you have the knowledge and tools to build your passive income portfolio, it is time to put them into practice. Start by following the step-by-step action plan outlined in Chapter 9 and build your first income stream. Whether you are investing in real estate, starting an online business, or diving into dividend stocks, take action today to start your journey.

Remember, the road to financial freedom is different for everyone. Some will focus on real estate, others will create content, while some might focus on dividend investing. The key is to remain consistent, stay open to learning, and always be on the lookout for new opportunities.

Final Words of Encouragement:

Building a passive income portfolio is a life-changing decision, and it is one that has the potential to create lasting wealth for you and your family. Financial freedom allows you the freedom to live life on your own terms, whether that means traveling the world, spending more time with loved ones, or pursuing your passions without the pressure of a 9-to-5 job.

Stay focused on your goals, keep pushing forward, and know that every step you take brings you closer to achieving the life you've always dreamed of.

Thank you for taking the time to read this book. I wish you the very best on your journey toward financial independence. You have the knowledge, the tools, and the drive to succeed—now it's time to take action and create your own path to freedom.

Thank you for reading, and I wish you all the best on your journey to financial freedom!

Acknowledgments

Writing this book has been an incredible journey, and I would not have been able to complete it without the support, guidance, and inspiration of many individuals.

First and foremost, I want to thank my family for their unwavering belief in me. Your encouragement and patience gave me the strength to pursue this project, even during the most challenging moments.

A heartfelt thank you to the mentors and teachers who have shaped my understanding of passive income and financial freedom. Your wisdom has been instrumental in helping me translate complex ideas into practical, actionable advice.

To my readers: this book is for you. Your curiosity and determination to take control of your financial future inspire me every day. I hope this book serves as a guide and a source of motivation as you embark on your journey toward financial independence.

Finally, I want to express my gratitude to the countless entrepreneurs, investors, and creators whose stories and strategies have paved the way for all of us. Your contributions to the world of passive income are a testament to what is possible with perseverance and vision.

Thank you all for making this book possible.

With gratitude,

FREQUENTLY ASKED QUESTIONS (FAQ)

1 How long does it take to build a reliable passive income stream?

The timeline varies depending on the method you choose. For example:

- Writing and selling an e-book can take a few weeks to months.
- Real estate investments may take a year or more to generate significant returns.
- Dividend-paying stocks require consistent investments over time to build a substantial portfolio.

Consistency, effort, and initial investment all play crucial roles in determining how quickly you see results.

2 Do I need a lot of money to start?

Not necessarily. Many passive income streams require little to no upfront capital:

- Starting a blog or YouTube channel may require only minimal investment in a domain or equipment.
- Affiliate marketing relies more on time and creativity than money.

For options like real estate or investing in stocks, you will need more capital, but starting small and reinvesting earnings can lead to growth.

3   Is passive income truly "passive"?

While the term implies little to no effort, most passive income streams require initial work to set up. For example:

- Writing an e-book requires upfront effort to create and publish the content.

- Real estate investing involves property research and management setup.

After this setup phase, the income becomes more passive, but occasional maintenance or updates are often necessary.

4   What are the biggest risks of passive income investments?

Some common risks include:

- **Market volatility:** Investments in stocks, real estate, or cryptocurrency can fluctuate in value.

- **Scams:** Be cautious of "get rich quick" schemes that promise high returns with little effort.

- **Poor time management:** Overcommitting to multiple projects can dilute your focus and lead to underperformance.

Minimizing risk involves thorough research, diversification, and seeking advice when needed.

5   How do I choose the best passive income stream for me?

Ask yourself:

- How much time can I invest upfront?
- What is my financial starting point?
- What are my skills and interests?

For instance, if you enjoy writing, creating digital products or starting a blog might be a good fit. If you have capital to invest, real estate or dividend stocks might suit your goals better.

6   Can passive income replace my 9-to-5 job?

Yes, but it takes time and planning. The key is to calculate your monthly expenses and create income streams that consistently cover those costs. A combination of diversified streams—such as rental income, dividends, and royalties—can provide stability and freedom from traditional employment.

7   Are there any tax implications I should know about?

Passive income is typically taxable. For example:

- Rental income is subject to property-related taxes.
- Dividends and investment income may be taxed based on your income bracket.

It is essential to consult with a tax professional or use tax software to ensure compliance and take advantage of deductions or credits.

8   How do I scale my passive income streams?

Scaling involves reinvesting your earnings into new or existing streams. For example:

- Use profits from a rental property to buy another property.

- Take revenue from an e-book and invest in creating an online course.

Automation, outsourcing, and leveraging technology can also help expand your efforts.

9   What are some beginner-friendly passive income ideas?

Here are a few options for beginners:

- Start a blog or YouTube channel.

- Sell print-on-demand products or stock photos.

- Invest in dividend-paying stocks or ETFs with low initial capital.

- Create digital products, such as e-books or templates, and sell them online.

- Rent out unused space (e.g., a garage, spare room, or parking spot).

These methods are accessible for those with limited time or resources and can grow into more significant streams over time.

10   What if one passive income stream fails?

Failure is always a possibility, but diversification minimizes the risk. By spreading your efforts and investments across multiple streams, a setback in one area will not significantly impact your overall financial health. For example:

- If your blog traffic declines, your investments in stocks or real estate can provide stability.

- Always be prepared to adapt and pivot when needed by staying informed and open to new opportunities.

11   How much time do I need to invest initially?

The initial time commitment depends on the type of passive income stream. Examples:

- Writing an e-book might take 20–50 hours of focused work.

- Setting up a rental property could take weeks for research, purchasing, and preparation.

- Launching a blog might take 10–15 hours to establish the basics, with ongoing work to create content and grow the audience.

12   How do I automate my passive income streams?

Automation tools can save you time and effort. Examples include:

- **For online stores:** Platforms like Shopify or Etsy handle transactions, inventory, and customer communication.

- **For blogs or websites:** Use tools like WordPress plugins for SEO and scheduling.

- **For investments:** Robo-advisors like Betterment or Acorns manage portfolios automatically.

Automation allows you to focus on expanding or diversifying while maintaining existing streams.

13   Can I build passive income while working full-time?

Absolutely. Many people start building passive income alongside their day job.

- Dedicate a few hours each week to creating or managing income streams.
- Use weekends or evenings to set up systems like digital products or investments.

The key is to start small and prioritize activities that yield the highest returns for your available time.

14   Are there passive income methods I can do with no skills?

Yes, some methods require minimal expertise to get started:

- Renting out items (e.g., tools, vehicles, or equipment) requires no special skills.
- Investing in index funds is a beginner-friendly way to grow wealth over time.
- Selling print-on-demand merchandise can be done using pre-made templates or designs.

Learning new skills over time can open up more advanced opportunities.

15   How do I stay motivated when building passive income?

Focus on your long-term goals and celebrate small milestones along the way. Passive income requires patience and persistence, especially in the early stages.

Surround yourself with like-minded individuals or join online communities to share progress and stay inspired.

16   Is passive income suitable for everyone?

While anyone can benefit from passive income, not all methods suit every individual. Consider:

- Your risk tolerance: High-risk options like cryptocurrency may not appeal to everyone.

- Your time and financial resources: Some methods require significant upfront commitment.

- Your personal interests: You are more likely to succeed with income streams aligned with your skills or passions.

The key is finding a method that resonates with your lifestyle and goals.

Glossary of Terms

Below is a glossary of common terms related to passive income and financial freedom to help readers better understand the concepts discussed in the book:

Active Income
Income earned directly through work or services, such as a salary, hourly wages, or freelance projects.

Affiliate Marketing
A business model where individuals earn a commission by promoting other people's products or services.

Assets
Resources owned by an individual or business that have economic value, such as real estate, stocks, or intellectual property.

Cash Flow
The movement of money in and out of a business or personal finances. Positive cash flow occurs when income exceeds expenses.

Compound Interest
Interest calculated on the initial principal and the accumulated interest from previous periods. This is a key principle in building wealth through investments.

Crowdfunding
The process of raising funds for a project or business from a large number of people, typically via online platforms.

Diversification
A risk management strategy that involves spreading investments across various asset classes to reduce the impact of a single loss.

Dividend
A portion of a company's earnings distributed to shareholders, often as a reward for investing in the company.

Equity
The ownership stake in an asset, such as real estate or a business, after liabilities are subtracted.

Financial Independence
A state where an individual's passive income is sufficient to cover their living expenses, eliminating the need for active work.

Intellectual Property (IP)
Creations of the mind, such as books, courses, or software, that can generate passive income through licensing or sales.

Passive Income
Income earned with minimal ongoing effort after the initial setup, such as rental income, royalties, or dividends.

Portfolio
A collection of financial assets, such as stocks, bonds, or real estate, owned by an individual or organization.

Return on Investment (ROI)
A performance measure used to evaluate the profitability of an investment, calculated as a percentage of the initial investment.

Scalability
The ability of a business model or income stream to grow without a significant increase in costs or effort.

Side Hustle
A secondary source of income outside of a primary job, often used to build passive income streams.

Stock
A type of security that represents ownership in a company and entitles the shareholder to a portion of its profits.

Upfront Investment
The initial time, money, or effort required to create a passive income stream before it begins generating revenue.

Wealth Building
The process of accumulating assets and investments over time to achieve financial security and independence.

Appendix: Resources for Further Learning

While this book has provided you with a comprehensive guide to getting started with passive income, there are many more resources available to deepen your knowledge. Below are a few resources you may find helpful:

1. **Books:**
   - *Rich Dad Poor Dad* by Robert Kiyosaki
   - *The Millionaire Fastlane* by MJ DeMarco
   - *The Lean Startup* by Eric Ries
   - *The Simple Path to Wealth* by JL Collins

2. **Websites and Blogs:**
   - *BiggerPockets* (for real estate investors)
   - *Smart Passive Income* by Pat Flynn
   - *The Motley Fool* (for stock investing)
   - *Neil Patel* (for digital marketing)

3. **Online Courses:**
   - *Udemy* offers various courses on passive income strategies, from real estate investing to starting an online business.

- *Coursera* and *Skillshare* offer courses on investing, entrepreneurship, and digital marketing.

- *BiggerPockets* also offers specialized real estate investing courses.

4. **Tools and Platforms:**

- **For Real Estate Investors:** Zillow, Realtor.com, Redfin for property research, and Fundrise for real estate crowdfunding.

- **For Stock Market Investors:** Robinhood, E*TRADE, and TD Ameritrade for brokerage accounts; Seeking Alpha for stock research.

- **For Online Businesses:** Shopify, WordPress, Clickfunnels, and Teachable for building and managing online businesses and courses.

- **For Passive Income Automation:** Zapier, Mailchimp, and ConvertKit for automating marketing and business tasks.

With these resources at your disposal, you are ready to dive even deeper into the world of passive income. Your journey toward financial independence starts now—take that first step, and you will soon be on your way to building a life of freedom and opportunity.

Bibliography and References

Books and Publications

- Kiyosaki, Robert T. *Rich Dad Poor Dad: What the Rich Teach Their Kids About Money That the Poor and Middle Class Do Not!*. Warner Books, 2000.
- Hill, Napoleon. *Think and Grow Rich*. The Ralston Society, 1937.
- Ferriss, Timothy. *The 4-Hour Workweek: Escape 9-5, Live Anywhere, and Join the New Rich*. Crown Publishers, 2007.
- Cardone, Grant. *The 10X Rule: The Only Difference Between Success and Failure*. Wiley, 2011.
- Bogle, John C. *The Little Book of Common Sense Investing: The Only Way to Guarantee Your Fair Share of Stock Market Returns*. Wiley, 2007.

Websites and Online Resources

- Investopedia. "Understanding Passive Income." https://www.investopedia.com
- BiggerPockets. "Real Estate Investing for Beginners." https://www.biggerpockets.com
- Shopify Blog. "How to Start a Print-on-Demand Business." https://www.shopify.com

- NerdWallet. "Best Dividend Stocks to Buy and Hold." https://www.nerdwallet.com
- Medium. "Passive Income Ideas for Beginners." https://www.medium.com

Articles and Reports

- Piketty, Thomas. "Capital in the Twenty-First Century." *Harvard University Press*, 2013.
- Financial Times. "The Rise of Passive Investing." *Financial Times*, 2020.
- Harvard Business Review. "The Truth About Passive Income." *HBR*, 2019.

Tools and Platforms Mentioned

- Amazon Kindle Direct Publishing (KDP). https://kdp.amazon.com
- Etsy for Sellers. https://www.etsy.com
- Acorns Investment App. https://www.acorns.com
- WordPress Blog Hosting. https://wordpress.org

Author's Final Note

As you reach the final pages of this book, I want to take a moment to remind you of the incredible potential within you. The journey to building passive income and achieving financial freedom is not a straight path—it is a road filled with learning, persistence, and growth.

You may encounter challenges along the way, and that is okay. Every obstacle you face is an opportunity to learn, adapt, and strengthen your resolve. Remember, the most successful people did not achieve their goals overnight. They started where they were, used what they had, and never gave up.

This book is not just a guide but a starting point. Use the knowledge you have gained here as a foundation to build the life you have envisioned. Experiment with different strategies, find what works for you, and do not hesitate to revisit and refine your approach as your circumstances evolve.

Above all, keep your "why" at the forefront. Whether it is financial security, more time with loved ones, or the freedom to pursue your passions, your purpose is your most powerful motivator.

Thank you for allowing me to be a part of your journey. I hope this book inspires you to take action, dream big, and create a future filled with opportunities and abundance. Your journey is uniquely yours, and I cannot wait to see what you will accomplish.

Wishing you success, fulfillment, and a life of financial freedom,

Aline Szpaller.

www.ingramcontent.com/pod-product-compliance
Lightning Source LLC
Chambersburg PA
CBHW071030240526
45469CB00006BD/2162